Meditation: The Path to Peace

Dr. Lisa Love

Ageless Publications
Ojai, CA.

Dr. Lisa Love
lisa@doctorlisalove.com

Pictures used in this book — public domain through Microsoft Publisher

Get help with the teachings in this book directly from Dr. Lisa Love.

To learn more about Coaching, Books, Seminars, Teleclasses visit:

Website:
www.doctorlisalove.com

Social Media:
www.facebook.com/drlisalove
www.twitter.com/doctorlisalove
www.youtube.com/doctorlisalove

"Learn to recognize the YOU in you, so you can attract to yourself who you *really* are."

Beyond the Secret:
Spiritual Power & the Low of Attraction
By Dr. Lisa Love

Table of Contents

Table of Contents, cont

Table of Contents, cont

Foreword

For most of my life meditation has been an important and nearly daily practice. My first encounters with meditation began when I was very young and started as a form of prayer. By age fifteen they were more evolved with me practicing the relaxation, visualization and self-hypnosis techniques that laid the foundation for my deeper experiences of meditation to come. In my mid-twenties my formal study of meditation began. At one point in my mid-twenties, I was so absorbed in meditation practice, I actually meditated four continuous hours a day for two years. By 1984 I was teaching meditation to others. I even had the honor in 1986 to teach meditation to a group of men suffering from AIDS as part of the *Inland Aids Project's* efforts to utilize meditation as a way of managing disease and stress.

Following this extensive period of intensified meditation training and teaching, I went through a number of mystical episodes in 1989 that radically altered my perception of myself and life. My deep need to understand what had happened to me led me into furthering my education beyond my traditional counseling degrees and during the next fifteen years I received more degrees in esoteric philosophy as well as spiritual and transpersonal psychology. During these years I expanded my research on meditation by delving into an understanding of how different spiritual and religious traditions viewed and pursued it.

During this time period I had a unique opportunity presented to me. In 1994 a then small start-up Internet company known as *America Online* was looking for people who would teach various topics in their newly formed Online Campus. I jumped at the opportunity and decided to share my passion for meditation in this new medium. There was only one major problem, how to do it? After all this was the era where much of the

Internet still existed on archaic bulletin board servers. Speed on the Internet was painfully slow. In fact, it was so slow that while I was listening to the hideous connection noise I would sing a song I made up called *The Waiting Song.* I would only stop singing minutes later when I at last heard the word "Welcome."

As for teaching online this was an era where the only way to teach was through chat rooms and bulletin boards. I wondered to myself how in the world I would teach meditation in such an environment? So I meditated and answers began to emerge. In fact, the solutions I innovated were so revolutionary at the time the head of the *America Online's* Online Campus asked me to teach over 200 of their now burgeoning campus teachers how to implement what I was pioneering.

The text in this book is actually then a compilation of various chat room transcript dialogues that I had with my students over the course of that first year. By 1995, I had shaped these transcripts up into book form and self-published the first version of this book using the major technology available to me at the time, *Kinkos*! For years I sold a few copies here and there all the while hoping that someday I might find the way to get the information I had complied about the benefits and practices of meditation out to a wider audience.

The reprinting of this book in 2011 marks that time period. Regarding the 2011 edition all the original text is intact with a few minor changes here and there. As a much more seasoned writer, I anticipated rewriting the entire book to reflect my new writing style, but decided instead to keep the majority of the book for the most part in its original form. That original form is packed with knowledge about meditation: what it is, what are it's benefits, and what are the basic methods for pursuing it.

I also contemplated expanding the book further by adding a variety of meditation exercises. I decided against this primarily because there are so many exercises I could include, I simply would not have room for them all. Also, meditation works best at first when others guide you through it. Like riding a bicycle, meditation is something you have *to do* to really learn about it. It is not something you can just read about. So, instead of just having you read mediations in this book, I encourage you to learn the basics about meditation given here. Then, if you want more assistance and instruction you can find a teacher or contact me directly to help you learn either by way of individual or group coaching. My website is www.doctorlisalove.com. There you will find information about all of my services including those that provide you with spiritual guidance and meditation training. And, in time you will also find a series of meditation workshops, CD's and videos created by me and those I partner with to assist you in your journey in deepening your understanding of who you are, and in helping you to improve your meditation practice. Blessings on your journey.

Dr. Lisa Love

Meditation: What is It?

You are about to learn one of the most powerful tools I know of — meditation! I've practiced various forms of meditation for over thirty years now. It is as much a staple of my life as food and water. I have even been known to say I don't think I could live without meditating on a daily basis. But what is meditation?

Less than fifty years ago the masses in the Western world viewed meditation as a mysterious process indulged in by mainly mystics, philosophers, and exotic Easterners. Many regarded it as an odd and quirky habit. Others believed only highly evolved beings took part in it. Overall, a great deal of misunderstanding and confusion existed amongst the general population. Today, the word meditation is common place. Best selling books promote it. Magazines have large subscriptions discussing the subject. Business people advocate meditation as part of their stress management programs. Even the word itself has fallen into a trite domain.

World wide the word meditation is used more frequently than ever.But, like the word love a general lack of understanding regarding the meaning, practice, and purpose of meditation still exists.What meditation is for one person, may be completely different for the next. Yet, both assume they know what the other speaks of when they claim to be meditating. Before beginning a meditation practice it is important to understand then, what exactly *is* meditation? What different kinds of meditation practices are there? What effects does meditation have? How do you know if you are successfully engaging in meditation? What do you hope to achieve by going through a meditation process? Which kinds of meditation practices will get you there? How do you meditate, including how do you overcome some of the difficulties that come up during meditation work? This book will attempt to help you better understand the answers to these questions.

To begin with let's look at the question — what is meditation? Starting with Webster's dictionary meditation is defined as an act of thinking, "especially close and continued thought." It is also "a form of private devotion consisting of deep, continued reflection on some religious theme." The word meditate can also be defined as, "contemplating, pondering, to intend or plan, to dwell in thought, to muse, reflect, and cogitate." There is also a reference synonym of "ponder." Looking at the loose definition of this word it appears that anyone engaged in the act of thinking is meditating; however, meditation is much more than this. An act of close and continued thought is involved. So is the process of reflection and even intention. And, this thought is related to the concept of devotion and often ultimately involves "religious themes."

> In its deepest sense meditation is a tool used for understanding deity. And, it is the means by which we learn to listen, interpret and correctly apply insights on the spiritual life into our daily life and affairs.

When put together meditation begins with the ability to reflect upon your various thoughts (and often the feelings and bodily associations connected to them). As you become more aware of your thought life, meditation helps you discipline your thought life in such a way you can sustain your focus upon one particular thought. As a spiritual practice this sustained focus further assists you as you learn to orient your mind to reflect upon and gain a deeper understanding of the nature of God,

Reality, or Spirit and your true purpose or reason for being alive. Taken further meditation goes beyond thought into a direct realization of the Divine including recognizing yourself as a divine being. Finally, meditation becomes a transformative tool where you alchemize the lower aspects of yourself into an increased translucent reflection of your Divine Self.

In its deepest sense meditation is a tool used for understanding deity. And, it is the means by which you learn to listen, interpret and correctly apply insights on the spiritual life into your daily life and affairs. This core definition is vital for you to grasp as we progress through this book since we will be discussing a great deal regarding meditation. The definition will also help you understand the proper implementation of various techniques that enhance the meditative process. It is important to note, however, that if at any time meditation techniques are separated from spiritual intention, they are reduced mainly to psychological reflection, methods of relaxation, and various methods of mind control, which may have little to do with a truly meditative state as defined in this book.

For the modern person, it is good to know that meditation also need not be attached to many of the things associated with it like long flowing robes, living in a cave or on top of a mountain, and rejecting everything related to living in the world (family, career, money, etc.). Nor do you have to sit and chant with a group of people, contort yourself into difficult physical postures, participate in strange looking rituals, or speak repetitively over prayer beads to meditate. Though these activities can supplement meditation, they are not necessary for effective meditation work. Keeping this in mind let's delve more into the meditation process.

Overview of Meditation Benefits

The benefits of meditation are numerous, which is why I can't wait to share some of them with you. Though some of these benefits only come with time and persistence, thankfully, many of these benefits are easy to cultivate. The important thing is to start with the basics and learn to get the benefits from them. Then, as you become a fan of meditation and realize the benefits, you will naturally desire to go from beginning to advanced meditation practices to help you actualize *all* of the benefits listed here. Let us briefly review them:

> Meditation involves an evolutionary process.
> It starts with a deliberate attempt to change your identity, to become that identity, and to be creative as that new identity.

Benefit One - Physical. One of the most noticeable and immediate effects of certain meditation techniques is the way they can calm the nervous system and put the muscles and body as a whole into a state of deep relaxation. When the body, brain, and nervous system are in a more deeply relaxed state they are better able to handle stress. In turn this helps to build up the immune system and inhibits the release of cortisone, the aging hormone, that is released during stress into the body. Meditation at this basic level is then an excellent tool for enhancing the health and vitality of the body and can even assist with preventing the early onset of aging.

Benefit Two - Emotional. It is also possible through meditation to learn to manage your emotions in such a way you gain insight into them and catch them at an early enough stage to transmute them into their more spiritual states. For example, as stated in my *Feeling Good and Living Great* book anger can be transmuted into energy, sorrow into compassion, jealousy into fulfillment, confusion into clarity, and happiness into joy. The more you learn to manage your emotions through meditative practices the greater will be your sense of poise even in difficult circumstances. And, with practice and persistence meditation can create a more consistent state of calm, joy, and optimism within your emotions allowing you to face life with greater courage and emotional awareness and intelligence.

Benefit Three - Mental. Meditation in many ways it a perfect antidote to the downside of Attention Deficit Disorder so prevalent today. Why? Because in can help you understand, focus, and concentrate your thoughts. Mindfulness techniques of meditation are especially useful in helping you be more aware of the flow of your thoughts and the environment. Here you can begin to develop what is often known as the "witness" consciousness, which involves the ability to objectively witness what is going on within you and around you in a compassionate and detached way.

Next, meditation at this level can help you focus and concentrate the mind. This makes it easier for you to reason things through in a clear and helpful way. And, it helps you see things more clearly as they really are. As you develop these perceptive qualities of the mind meditation improves your capacity for discernment allowing you to mentally sort through what is and is not healthy for your spiritual well being in the short term and long term in your life.

Finally, meditation at this level can help you still the flow of thoughts altogether bestowing in time a tranquil quiet and reflective capacity in the mind that can bring about a profound peace of mind as you learn to quiet the mind, while keeping it awake and alert. Now, the mind is simply the tool of your higher spiritual self, which uses the mind increasingly as a reflective lens through which to observe the world.

Benefit Four - Personal. The more adept you become at the first three levels of meditation, the more you can turn your attention to using meditation to help you coordinate your thinking, feeling, and acting so they are in sync. Too many times in life your goals and intentions may not work out. Frequently, this is because you are not coordinating your thoughts, feelings, and actions in such a way they no longer sabotage your success. For example, maybe you have carefully thought something through, but you lack the emotional or physical energy to carry out those thoughts. Meditation at this level is the remedy for this and there are specific techniques that aid this process.

Benefit Five - Spiritual. Advanced meditation practices go beyond the personal and have the effect of helping you change your way of behaving so you no longer act as an egotistical person. Instead, you behave like someone who is more awake and receptive to the love, light, and power of your higher self, or soul. As you become aware of the soul's presence and learn about soulful ways of being, you can internalize those qualities during a meditation process and begin to alchemize yourself consciously into becoming a more soulful individual.

Benefit Six - Universal. As you progress into more advanced meditation practices the techniques at this level are meant to help you expand your consciousness into wider and wider realms of Being. The more conscious you become of the world around you and within you, the more meditation will allow you to experience yourself as at-one with all that is. This realization of at-one-ment will not be just a spiritual platitude, it will be a deep ever present palpable realization that in turn reorients your entire value system and reason for being in this world. Now you will possess a deep motivation and drive to become a good steward of life, and an agent of love, light, and spiritual power throughout the world.

Benefit Seven - Transformational. As you may realize the more you meditate, especially using more and more advanced techniques, the more your sense of "I" will grow and expand. In many ways it will begin to seem as if the real "you" is looking down into your thoughts, feelings, and body in an increasingly compassionate, yet insistent way. What the new "you" will be insisting is that you constantly change your thoughts, feelings and even the nature of your physical habits and physical biology, so that you can alchemize yourself into becoming a whole new person.

This new person, or "I", will be a truer reflection of the spiritual you. Identified as the spiritual "I" you will be better able to live in the moment, enjoy the world, and respond to others with greater wisdom and love. In many ways you will be like the caterpillar who has transformed into a butterfly. And, meditation is the best tool I know of to help you get there.

Benefit Eight - Creative. What makes someone a genius? For the most part it is the fact that the individual is highly creative and continually open to new insights. For this reason he or she is able to "genesis" or create something new that others have not seen of or thought of before. Meditation helps this creative process because as your body is still, your emotions calm, and your mind is concentrated, focused, and alert you are better able to access creative insights and inspirations.

Combined with the benefits of coordination of the personality, meditation assists the creative process because it helps you to become a more stable and productive (i.e. creative) human being. But, at an even higher level meditation (as mentioned in the previous benefit) allows you in many ways to re-create, or create, yourself! As a "conscious soul incarnate," meditation allows you to become a creative force for good in the world. Conscious, soulful, and present you are increasingly given the spiritual power to recreate the world with your creative skills so that soulful qualities (such as beauty, truth, wisdom, and compassion) are regularly used to help the world become a more loving and spiritual place.

So why meditate? Because as I have just revealed the benefits are enormous. That is why I often tell people I would rather go without food than live without meditation. As you meditate many of these benefits will become evident right away. Others will only emerge as your meditation practice is deepened through a prolonged period of time. With all these benefits no wonder many truly creative and spiritual people throughout history practice meditation. Meditation can transform the world into an entirely new way of being. And, it can reveal the true nature of Spirit, including the essential spiritual immortality you possess within you, which is a very liberating experience. Ultimately, meditation can also bring you a fierce, but compassionate courage. As it removes fear (even the fear of death), and bestows upon you greater peace, it can help you live each and every day in a state of love, light, bliss and joy.

Physical & Emotional Benefits

PHYSICAL BENEFITS

<u>Benefit One.</u> Producing a reasonable amount of physical well-being so there is health and vitality in the physical instrument.

At the time of your birth you were given a marvelous physical instrument. And, that physical body allows you to do the many things you desire. With an amazing amount of complexity and resiliency your physical body is impacted every day by all the stresses and pleasures of life. Through it all your body does it's best to sustain you through your life without breaking down. Because your body tends to be such a wonderful servant, it is easy to take it for granted. Regardless, it is important to learn to maximize the potential of your body so that it can be more vital, flexible, and free from debilitating disease.

Along these lines meditation can help you. It can enable you to have a healthy and vital physical body in a number of ways. Whenever you meditate you are attempting to bring conscious awareness to something. When applied to the body, meditation helps you gain a reasonable understanding of your body, how it works, and its needs and wants. The more you understand these things the more you will be motivated to gain insight into your body, so it can assist you by being a healthy benefactor throughout your life.

When meditation is applied to the body one of the most noticeable impacts is learning how to quickly reduce the impacts of stress. Stress is best defined as the amount of pressure or exertion something must sustain. Looked at in this way you can see how you are always under stress of some kind. Healthy stress is knowing how to create just the right amount of pressure or exertion to make your life challenging, adventuresome, and rewarding. Unhealthy stress happens with undue and often unrelenting nervous excitation that in time leads to greater irritability, fatigue, lethargy, anxiety, and even disease.

When meditation is used as a tool in the reduction of stress, it is primarily a method to calm nervous excitation and facilitate a relaxation response. As you learn to relax the body through progressive steps you also become increasingly aware as to where and how tension is stored in your body. This tension is then released by consciously manipulating the muscular system by progressively isolating the various muscle groups within the body so that you can direct each one to relax. As the muscles relax they in turn improve circulation and release nervous tension (especially when you are relaxing the surrounding tissue around the nerves which may be inadvertently pinched, or stressed by tense muscles). With skill, relaxation techniques can regularly refresh you throughout the day giving you mini-breaks of relaxation. Or, they can move you into a deep state of relaxation, even at times putting you to sleep in the process.

Meditation in relation to the physical body may further be used to assist in the healing of the physical body itself. On the simplest level, meditation brings about insights as to what is ailing the physical body, and regarding what ameliorative methods might best cure it. On a more profound level meditation teaches you sensitivity to your body's mechanisms, even to the extent where bodily organs and functions can be consciously manipulated at will. This later statement need not surprise you. As all of us mature from infancy to adulthood many of our biological functions come under automatic control based upon the pre-programming found in the genetic structure. Meditation practices here are a furthering of this process as you learn to bring bodily functions under more conscious control.

Though genetics and early childhood programming can incline you towards a certain physical destiny, with conscious awareness, you need not be locked into certain physical patterns. You can learn to consciously change them. With tools such as biofeedback you can even learn to consciously monitor and change your breathing, heartbeat, and so forth. You might also learn how to reduce symptoms of bodily pain. Taken to the furthest extent, even debilitating diseases can themselves be healed as you gain insight into methods that will help you work more effectively with your physical body organism.

A final way meditation benefits the physical body, is through insights that allow you to cope effectively regarding any perceived limitations you may come across should an ailing or handicapped physical body befall you. Here meditation can reveal to you through a process of mental training and proper identification that although your body is important to your well being in life, it is not your true identity. You learn that although you have a body, you are not your physical body. You are much more than this. As you free yourself from the belief that the body is your essential being in life, you can discover that a deep, rich, rewarding life can still be open to you especially as you learn to access higher levels of spiritual Self-expression.

As you free yourself from the belief that the body is your essential being a rich and rewarding life opens to you through learning to access higher levels of spiritual Self-expression.

Benefits, Exercise One: Pause for a moment. Spend at least five minutes becoming aware of your amazing physical body and all its various parts including: head, arms, legs, torso, circulatory system, nervous system, muscles, bones, organs of all kinds. Bring into conscious awareness as much as you are able to regarding your physical body. Attempt to do this without judgment. Simply appreciate all that your body does for you. Marvel at how willingly it has served you, even when you disregarded and abused it. Consider the billions of cells struggling daily to rejuvenate and restore you. Then shift your focus to the bodily organs doing their best to withstand the impact of the environment so they might remain at full optimum potential. See your body as a cherished friend, who has served you silently for all these years. Acknowledge and appreciate it. Send all parts of it your best. And, as much as possible embrace every wonderful beautiful inch of your body — the precious house you live in.

EMOTIONAL BENEFITS

Benefit Two. Creating a state of calm, joy, and optimism in the emotional instrument so problems and opportunities can be faced with courage and right action.

Even though your physical body may be fit, it does you precious little good if you are beset by numerous chaotic emotions. An emotion is fundamentally the motion, or movement, into visible manifestation of a sentient feeling sensation. You can feel or sense many things. In meditation practices emotions are often equated symbolically with water.

That is why you may hear people describe their emotions as turbulent, stormy, steamy, and so forth. In meditation practice it is good to view the emotions as a clear calm pool of water indicating that they are calm and serene.

> As you calm the emotions in meditation practice you are much better able to reflect on your true identity as Spirit. The more you remember who you really are as a spiritual being, the easier it will be to move through the passage of life with confidence, joy, and optimism.

As you calm the emotions in meditation practice you are then much better able to reflect on your true identity as Spirit. The more you remember who you really are as a spiritual being, the easier it will be to move through the passage of life with confidence, joy, and optimism. But, these emotional states cannot be falsely induced. To be real they must rest upon a deep inner security. This inner security emerges from a set of principles which are timeless, eternal, and of true worth in your life, and meditation will help reveal these principles to you. Also, in meditation your feeling nature can be trained to reach out and sense what is most essential. You can understand better what is worth living for and worth dying for. You can also become more attuned to where you need to love and be loved more in your life and discover in meditation how to access both. Such is the profound mystery of your feeling body and the innate wisdom of your emotional needs.

In the broadest sense emotions are primarily reactions to either pleasure or pain. For many, mastery over the state of their emotions is much more difficult than what is required over the physical instrument. Though emotions when genuine and constructively handled serve you, when misdirected they cause difficulties. For example, undue grief and suffering can debilitate all your outer efforts to accomplish what you may really want in life or to live each day in a tranquil and happy state. Uncontrolled anger can inhibit or majorly block opportunities for success because you are unwittingly alienating others. Anxiety and worry may cause you to hold back and delay appropriate action. Confusion may induce paranoia and a variety of fears as you fail to see your way clearly into intelligent action. Hostility may harden you and block your chance to be a recipient of compassion. Over-confidence may create arrogance and keep you from recognizing your impending downfall.

More than likely you know what it is like to fall victim to misdirected emotions. The sign that you have failed to effectively channel them in a positive direction is how much worse you may feel after you have handled them poorly. At the same time it does no good to suppress emotions because suppression can create just as many difficulties. As my book *Feeling Good & Living Great* reveals feelings are important. The secret is to learn to work with your feelings well. Then they will help you sense and work within your environment effectively.

When you misjudge what is happening with others around you and deny your and their real feelings, you may act foolishly. An example is when you don't assert your anger in a healthy way by setting a boundary on someone disrespecting you. Then, that person may end up taking advantage of you, or feel it is alright to harm you in some way. Another example is when you fail to pay attention to your fear when it may be attempting to alert you to the fact that an impending danger is present. In either case you are victimized time and again by not handling your emotions well.

Listening and paying attention to the emotions, while at the same time respecting the higher processes of reason is the secret to your eventual success in working with emotions well. How can meditation help this? Meditation exercises in relation to emotions help you identify and then consciously alter your emotional states at will. This is not a false covering up, but rather a constant remembering of who you really are beyond any emotional state. From this state of awareness a calm knowing emerges that you can face any outward circumstances if you approach them as your highest and best Self.

Again, meditation allows you to become conscious of yourself and your environment. When faced with the two broad categories of feeling states, those of pleasure and pain, meditation helps you work with each in an effective way. In regards to emotional pain, meditation allows you to heal it with compassion and understanding. By observing the content of your thoughts and the events that created the painful emotions you gain insight. And, you learn to choose different feeling states, or recreate the events in your mind so that you can imagine them having resolved in a more positive way. Upon doing this you in turn reprogram memories stored within the brain so that they do not create the same kind of triggers when touched on in similar situations. And, you condition yourself to react with a healthier emotional responses should similar events arise in the future.

As for emotions attached to pleasurable states in your life, you can program yourself to more consciously focus upon and remember events in your life that help you feel good, not just bad. Focusing on positive emotions helps you select for them. And, the more you can consciously use meditation to help you enhance positive emotional states, the more you can cultivate a positive storehouse of emotional energy to help you feel good throughout life, and to help you cope better when events are difficult.

In both the practice of reprogramming painful emotional events and enhancing pleasurable ones the meditation methods that are often most effective are visualizations. Visualizations are also useful in the creative meditation process. But, again in regards to emotions they help you to consciously replace painful emotions and memories with pleasant ones. Going on guided journeys where you walk through a path in nature, entering a spiritual building like a church or temple, or coming into contact with a spiritual being and having a conversation with that person all examples of meditation used at the emotional level.

Other meditation techniques that can help with emotions are those that include breathing exercises. By stilling or redirecting the breath you can make use of the mind/body connection to help you bring certain emotions under more conscious control. Breathing calms down the nervous system. As your body calms down, your emotions calm down. From that space you will be able to think more calmly and rationally concerning how to act upon any feeling sensation you are currently involved with. Combined with a deeper understanding of how to consciously work with various emotional states well, you can then move through your life in a state of greater emotional clarity and peace.

Benefits, Exercise Two. Again, pause and consider for a minimum of five minutes the two broad categories of feeling states — pleasure and pain. Spend five minutes thinking about painful emotional states, then switch and spend five minutes reflecting on the pleasurable ones. Notice how at will you can consciously switch from one state of emotions to the next.

Refine these categories even further into subtle levels. For example, pleasure can bring joy, excitement, enthusiasm, content, and so forth. Pain can bring frustration, sorrow, anger, grief, etc. Knowing this move again from pleasure to pain, and then from pain to pleasure again. Notice how as you do you can learn to become ever more sensitive to, and at choice about, various feeling states.

Now recognize how you typically act upon various feeling states. How intense are you with certain emotions? How suppressed? How conscious are you of your emotional impact on yourself and others? Be careful to simply observe what is so without judgment. Simply learn at this point to honor the power of your emotions; honor the sensitivity of your feeling nature. Then close by affirming that you, as your essential spiritual Self, can consciously and intelligently direct the feeling and emotional states in your life.

Mental & Personal Benefits

As you progress in understanding the benefits of meditation you move beyond those related simply to the body and emotions. Likewise, you move from more simplistic meditation experiences to those at a more intermediate level where the benefits deal primarily with the mind and the overall coordination of your three-fold instrument (mind, emotions, physical nature).

MENTAL BENEFITS

Benefit Three. Bringing peace of mind, discrimination, and mindfulness to the mental faculties so life can be seen clearly, allowing for reasonable and correct evaluation of reality.

Your mind is a powerful tool. Whether you are conscious of it or not every moment of every day thoughts of all kinds are endlessly pouring through your mind. Occasionally you may catch some of these thoughts and focus on them. Normally, these thoughts pertain to your likes and dislikes, desires and disappointments. Thoughts here act more as interpretations of your feeling states and impulsive desires. For this reason, some Eastern teachings speak of thoughts as "kama-manas" or being comprised of the "desire mind" " (kama meaning desire, manas meaning mind). A mind that stays at this level is primarily emotional in nature. These emotions need not be angry, despairing, or dark. They can be highly idealistic. Still, they do not reflect higher levels of thought because whether coming from a higher or lower emotional state these so-called thoughts are mostly emotionally driven and not very likely to be clear, well thought-out, and organized.

When certain meditative techniques are applied this begins to change. As you calm your physical and emotional bodies down into a state of rest, you are now freed up to more consciously observe the contents of your thought life. Now, any focus on your body or emotions (including imagined journeys) need to drop away. Then meditation practices at this level shift your focus more towards your ability to simply observe or witness your thoughts as they pass by. Or they may focus on cultivating the capacity to concentrate your thoughts in a particular direction. They may even encourage you to quiet your thoughts completely.

When you first sit down and try to still your mind you might run into is how active your mind is to begin with. You might also observe that your mind jumps from thought to thought to thought. This tendency of the mind to jump around is often referred to as the "monkey mind" because the mind is not only jumping around from thought to thought as if it is leaping from tree to tree to tree; the mind is constantly chattering like a monkey. Of the two methods just mentioned (concentrating the mind or observing it), observing the mind is typically the easiest method to try at first. And, one of the major benefits of observing the contents of your thoughts is learning to do so without judgment. Rather, you simply see your thoughts coming and going like clouds passing by above you, curious as to what lies there in a compassionate and dispassionate way.

Meditations that involve observing your thoughts are often known as mindfulness meditations and they can be quite demanding for many people. If you are a beginner to meditation practice you may often be surprised at the content of your thought life and may become very reactive, distracted, and judgmental in relation to those thoughts. But, as you get accustomed to observing the flow of your thoughts you can go a step further. Now, you can inquire as to the origin of these thoughts and discover a great deal about your conditioning to think along certain lines. For example, you may ask yourself how much of what you think is something you consciously want to think? Or how much of it based upon programming from your childhood, society, and so forth? Have you really questioned what you think and why? How much of this is based upon belief vs. actual experience? How do you know what you know? How much of what you know is really true? How do you know what is truth to begin with? As you consider these questions you will also discover why so many advanced practitioners of meditation become reflective, highly intelligent, visionary, and creative leaders in their various fields of endeavors, because you will become one as well.

In time, you can learn to not only observe your thoughts and inquire into them, you will learn how to gain mastery over them. Mental practices for meditation shift at this stage away from allowing any and every thought to come into your mind, towards learning how to bring your mind at will into a sharp, clear and concentrated focus along certain lines. Practices that involve concentrated effort by thinking along certain lines, especially what is known as a "seed thought" are frequently used here. A "seed thought" is a word or phrase that you "seed" into your mind so that you can concentrate your mind on that thought until insight occurs regarding what you are thinking about. The better you are at focusing on a seed thought the more you will develop discrimination and clarity as to the nature of your thinking, and mastery over your thoughts altogether. And, your perceptions regarding what others are thinking will become sharper giving you greater clarity regarding what is going on around you. Instead of the mind masking and clouding reality, it now becomes a powerful tool to more accurately reflect it.

> Meditation at this stage facilitates the shift from any and every thought coming into your mind, towards the power to bring the mind into a sharp and clear focus.

When your mind is not able to see reality clearly, it succumbs to deception, illusion, and closed mindedness. It is not able to think holistically by being able to see many points of view and hold them together in an inclusive whole with greater perspective and insight. For this reason your mind becomes one-sided or lop-sided making it less able to act as a tool to help you discipline and direct your emotions along positive and healing lines. And, your mind is not able to give you the insights you need to access knowledge to help in healing at any level including physical ailments. Finally, when you are unable to focus and direct your mind appropriately you will not be able to take advantage of higher opportunities for full life expression. That is because more fulfilling ways of living only open up to you when your mind is free from arrogance, rigidness, flightiness, and confusion.

After you master to some degree the discipline of being able to hold the mind in a concentrated way on one specific thought or object at a time, you can move to the next step of cultivating mental stillness. The more you enter into the silence the greater will be your capacity to shut your mind on and off by way of your directed will. Now, rambling and even obsessive/

fixated thoughts will cease. Your mind will enter into a greater level of peace staying quiet not only throughout the day, but even in your sleep as you more rapidly enter into deep dreamless sleep, which is similar to being at a high meditative state.

In this increased state of quiet your mind becomes increasingly like a mirror remaining silent and aware as it observes and pays full attention to the present moment. It also becomes keenly perceptive allowing it to discern what is most essential and important in any situation. Knowing how to do this with your mind you are now able to better determine and implement directions in your life that enable you to succeed at whatever you set out to do. And, from a more spiritual level, because you see the whole of reality more clearly with greater inclusivity and compassion, what you set out to do will be more oriented towards living a life of service where you attempt to be selfless, harmless, and compassionate in the use of your mind so it increasingly unifies instead of divides.

Benefit Exercise, Three: Pause to consider the nature of your thinking. Spend five minutes to observe your various thoughts. Do not censor your thinking. Allow every thought which appears to have its place. Simply observe it, then let it go. After a short time, ask yourself the following question: How much of what you are thinking represents the way you really wish to think? Realizing this appreciate that with skill and training you can over time, learn to master and constructively condition and direct the nature of your thought life.

> Naturally as these fruits are combined a growing sense of power, confidence, and charisma may emerge throughout your overall personality.

PERSONAL BENEFITS

Benefit Four. Coordinating the thinking, feeling, and acting components of an individual so he or she can more effectively carry out specific goals and intentions.

This benefit of meditation practice increases the level of self-mastery and free-will you will have over your life. Thus far, the benefits of meditation examined have all been designed to teach you to discipline and direct more consciously your thoughts, feelings, and actions. Now, these three components are brought together in a coordinated effort. Accomplishing this helps you mature into a person who can be congruent in your actions. In short, you walk your talk. The more you are able to do this, the more capable you will be in the attainment of your specified goals or ambitions. You will possess a certain level of one-pointed direction in relation to your chosen goals and the directions you want to pursue. And, at the same time, the openness and flexibility of your mind will remain. Because of this flexibility even if you have to divert your life path or attention temporarily to clear up some karma or bring something else into fruition as a preliminary step, doing so will not cause you to waver from your accomplishing your goal eventually.

As you reach this stage you will experience your mind, emotions and body differently. More than ever before you will have a clear mind capable of organizing and constructing a plan of action. Because your mind is increasingly sharp and penetrating without being close-minded or cruel, you will be able to anticipate, perceive, and cut through obstacles surfacing along the way without alienating others in the process. As for your emotions, more often than not they will remain calm and controlled. A sense of peace will pervade them. Your issues that stem from past traumas, bouts of anger, jealousy, depression, rage, hysteria, and over-enthusiasm will be regulated and subdued. If any of these emotions do surface, you will readily deal with them with the right amount of love, compassion, and clarity to help them heal.

Your emotional body will also possess a sufficient degree of sensitivity to the needs of others. This results in a general radiation of love and concern not only for yourself, but increasingly a wider circle of others around you. Care is taken that your emotions are not so oversensitive you tend to ignore the suffering of others because you cannot handle their suffering without being submerged. That's because when you are too sensitive you take on others problems as if they are your own. In doing so you lose a sense of solidity and a sense of your own distinct identity in the emotional field. Your issues then get blurred with the problems of others as if you are drowning in the waters with them. This over-identifying with the problems of others is quite different from an emotional state where you remain calm, poised, loving, yet detached enough to create an effective "rescue."

Finally, your physical nature will be increasingly regulated and consciously controlled in order to maintain its general health. Even if it is handicapped or debilitated with some physical difficulty, you will possess enough stamina and coordination to execute efficiently the plans of your mind, the aspirations of your emotions, and the overall goals of your entire persona. The various aspects of meditation practice referred to as relaxation, concentration, and some levels of visualization will be regularly implemented along these lines in order to bring these benefits about and to maintain them.

Naturally as these fruits are combined you will find yourself freer and even more desirous to pursue more advanced meditation work. A growing sense of power, confidence, and charisma may emerge throughout your overall personality. An accurate assessment of your talents and how to best implement them will be seen. A byproduct of this is the emergence of personal ambition, which may be either positive or negative. In a positive vein, the plans and goals you pursue will be implemented to help uplift and serve growing numbers of people, not just yourself. In a negative sense, you will be diverted into the ego and then even the tools of meditation practice may be used to fulfill selfish and self-serving ends. These include using your growing powers primarily to achieve wealth, fame, and personal success. Though acquiring wealth, fame, and personal success may at some point be a part of your life, to actively seek them out only for your own personal gain, drops the focus, and can cause you to become spiritually diverted until the selfish motivating factors within your personality are recognized and redirected into higher spiritual work.

At this stage you will also be increasingly attracted to the implementation of creative meditation practices. When applied selfishly, these tools are used to help people "create and have whatever they want out of life." This stems usually from a selfish motivation and is frequently evidence that someone has not pursued meditative or spiritual practices at the higher level. It will not be uncommon then to hear people say things like, "So long as it feels good, go for it." "He who dies with the most toys wins." "Look out for Number #1."

As of 2011 (the date for the second edition of this book) these phrases have become increasingly more popular and are have even been clumped under what are now known as "law of attraction" teachings. Yet, as I revealed in my best-selling *Beyond the Secret: Spiritual Power and the Law of Attraction* creative meditation practices often lack a spiritual motivation. Because people start to reap the fruits of meditation at this stage and these fruits seem so personally rewarding, many people stop at this level, failing to move beyond using so-called spiritual practices, stopping instead at the level of self-mastery and personal power. Feeling powerful due to the high level of self-mastery gained it is common to use meditation techniques mainly as a tool to go after what ever you want. And usually, at this stage you will be highly successful in doing so. However, when you come from personal power instead of spiritual power at some point things will go sour. Then you will be forced to reap the karma of selfish motivations, while giving you the opportunity to move on to even more advanced meditation practices to remedy the very same selfish motivations that emerged.

On another note, it is also not uncommon when arriving at this level to imbue your meditation process with religious tones that are the same time full of ambition to use the growing power and mastery you feel primarily for personal gain. Again this is personal power, it is not truly spiritual power, even though your words have a religious bent and the egotistical element may be harder to recognize. Instead, it is a form of spiritual materialism, where you cloak your desires to get whatever you want in spiritual language in an to attempt to make yourself feel good about what are basically selfish pursuits.

Another form of spiritual materialism is to use the religious aspect to help you gain a sense of power by ensuring you are part of the "in group," the "right group," or one of the "chosen ones" in the world. Here only the happiness of yourself or your group matters and the suffering in the world is often either deliberately ignored, rarely contemplated, or only alleviated because you hope to gain some spiritual brownie points in doing so. Even if you are not overtly spiritual but agnostic or atheistic, if you are on a quest for personal power and become hedonistic, enjoying life to the fullest at everyone else's expense, then you will run into difficulties eventually.

Again, meditation techniques at this level may help you achieve your personal hopes and ambitions, but they can also tempt you to become selfish and self-indulgent. Still, all this eventually turns towards the good when your selfish needs and desires burn out, because you are learning the negative lessons associated with selfish pursuits. Arriving at this point you will now be ready for the higher levels of meditative work.

Benefit Four: Exercise. Pause, and consider the following for a minimum of five minutes. Ask yourself, "What is my purpose in life?" "What goals have I established which help me accomplish this?" If you do not have a sense of overall purpose ask yourself, "Why not?" "How can I remedy this?" If you do have a purpose, consider how effective you are in reaching it.

Spiritual & Universal Benefits

We arrive now at the benefits of meditation practice, that allow you to penetrate into truly spiritual realms. The word spiritual is used in a number of different ways, but in this book it implies possessing a certain state of being that expresses itself as maturity, wisdom, compassion, intelligence, and selflessness in relation to your interaction with others. The word spiritual used here also represents a realization of the factual nature of immortality. This realization carries with it additional insights regarding your unity with all of life around you.

These spiritual understandings of immortality and unity achieved through meditation instill in you a deep desire to act on that realization through the effort to alleviate the suffering of not just yourself, but all sentient beings. That is one reason you begin to consciously rearrange your life so that you might become increasingly harmless in your thoughts, words, emotional reactions and deeds. Service also becomes a major focal point as all that you do is oriented towards using all of your gifts, talents, and resources to benefit others. And, you refine your motives so that they are increasingly selfless in nature.

SPIRITUAL BENEFITS

Benefit Five. Changing the identification of the individual from an egotistical focus, towards awakening and becoming receptive to the identity of being a soul.

As seen you can live a masterful and powerful life as you work with the benefits that meditative disciplines can give you. However, meditation doesn't really begin its *spiritual work* until you move far beyond the urge for personal mastery or power.

Anyone who has achieved much in the way of fame, wealth, and power realizes despite all the personal fulfillments that these bring emptiness can still surface. As it does a crisis as to the true meaning or purpose for being alive on this planet can ensue. Then the following question becomes relevant — if personal success cannot satisfy, then quite frankly what can?

Many people in life never reach the stage where they will experience this crisis. But, for those who do, a spark within is produced. This spark is best summarized in a powerful and relevant phrase from the Christian Bible, a passage that deals with the crisis of personal achievement, and the call for something more.

"If I speak in the tongues of men and of angels, but have not love, I am a noisy gong or a clanging cymbal. And, if I have prophetic powers, and understand all mysteries and all knowledge, and if I have all faith, so as to remove mountains, but have not love, I am nothing. If I give away all I have, and if I deliver my body to be burned, but have not love, I gain nothing. Love is patient and kind; love is not jealous or boastful; it is not arrogant or rude. Love does not insist on its own way; it is not irritable or resentful; it does not rejoice in wrong, but rejoices in the right. Love bears all things, believes all things, hopes all things, endures all things... So faith, hope, love abide, these three; but the greatest of these is love. Corinthians 13, Vs. 1-7 & 13."

This passage, so well used by many, and so little understood or followed by most, is the keynote for the next stage of development. This is the stage of soul awareness and soul growth. It is this stage of becoming and being a soul through the embodiment of soulful qualities, which meditation at this level helps you master. As a spiritual discipline, meditation makes the person who is singularly individual and self-serving aware of a different dimension of being. Within this new level that person begins to embody not only love, but something best represented by the phrase group consciousness. Group consciousness is awareness that you are not a disconnected individual, but part of a larger group. Through meditation that group expands more and more. Now, you become increasingly aware of others' needs and strive to view life through their eyes, not only your own.

> When you become aware of others and seek to understand their needs and life view through their eyes, you shift your exclusive orientation and awaken to the deeper levels of your spiritual self, or soul.

The awakening to your identity as a soul is is actually the first most spiritual and valuable component of the meditation practices discussed thus far. This shift represents a change from concern over gratifying just yourself, towards under-standing how best you can serve and meet the needs of others. Slowly, you realize you play only a small part in the world around you. You extend your vision. As you do your sense of the group widens as well as your feeling of interconnection with groups around you. Typically, the first group you identify with is your immediate circle of family and friends. But, as you continue to expand you identify with your community, country, the planet, and the cosmos as a whole. Now instead of trying to force the world to meet your demands, wishes, and desires you ask how you might meet the demands, wishes and desires of larger and larger groups through service in an intelligent and compassionate manner. Thus you become what is called a soul infused persona or the conscious soul incarnate (one who had consciously incarnated into everyday life soulful living).

What is the soul? The word soul is often viewed as an abstract term used to signify an entity of some kind out there that you need to contact. Often in the beginning stages of spiritual development it is natural to relate to the soul in this fashion. But, the soul is not really out there at all. Rather, it represents a conglomerate of certain qualities that you are seeking to tap into and express in here, within yourself, so that you become soulful in your everyday life. You become loving and wise, intelligent and clear, creative and proficient, generous and noble, compassionate and inclusive (to name just a few soulful qualities). The more soul like you are, the more others will notice it. Yes, on the surface they may look at you and see simply Jane Doe or Peter Fox. But, beneath that they will sense something profoundly different about you. Regardless of your outer appearance something about you will appeal to them on a deeper level, even if at first they don't know how to explain it.

As you seek to reveal and express the soul it becomes more joyful and peaceful, but it will not necessarily be stress and problem free. Stress and conflict are part of the everyday world. People may or may not always agree with you. They may or may not agree with or be supportive of your soul yearnings. Despite this you do your best to live within the light of your soul. If they are supportive consider yourself fortunate. If they are not, treat them soulfully regardless by attempting to respect them and their opinions.

Remember a soul relationship creates a harmonious interplay between two or more beings. Even when others oppose you or hurt you, you strive to hold others in a state of compassion and love. Meditation at this level aids your capacity to do this. Through meditation you consistently orient your thoughts, feelings, and actions toward understanding others. You strive to use your mind and intelligence to serve others in a skillful way. You use your feelings to create empathy, compassion, and concern. And, you use your actions to be positive, constructive, and harmless in all that you do. Step by step, bit by bit, the soul blossoms forth. You become a radiant point of light, love, and power. Your will is the will for the good. That way increasingly everything you do, think, feel, and say is oriented towards the skillful and wise service of another. You feel good by doing good and strive to sacrifice and serve with a joyful heart as you seek to make a difference in order to create a better world.

Benefits, Exercise Five: Pause and consider. "What does it mean to live as soul in my life?" "How often do my thoughts, feelings, actions express loving concern for others?" "How often do I seek to cultivate the qualities of compassion, harmlessness, and joy in what I do?" "How can I learn to use my talents for the sake of service in relation to others?" Now affirm to yourself, "I am the soul here and now." Slowly, become aware of what this affirmation means. How do you think differently, feel differently, and act differently when you are living as a soul?

UNIVERSAL BENEFITS

Benefit Six. Producing continual transferences of identity so the individual continues to expand in conscious awareness.

As you progress in spiritual practice you become increasingly aware of how meditation induces dramatic changes in the ways in which you operate and see yourself and the world around you. Suddenly or gradually you open up to new realities and dimensions you may not have considered before. The catalyst for making these changes can happen in a variety of ways. They may occur because a seemingly outer agent or event appeared to cause them. Examples include: undergoing a traumatic episode, a peak experience, having a vision, meeting a spiritual teacher, or using certain drugs that alter your awareness. These outer methods can give you fleeting insights into other ways of being. They can also create sudden and radical changes in your life as you discover that your perception of yourself and the world will never again be the same.

Though these outer events are often dramatic and at times intense, they usually do not last. Frequently, they can even create some confusion in your life as you seek to both understand and integrate what has been experienced and learned during these events. And, though they are significant it is important to note that there is much more to spiritual development than going through mystical episodes, ecstatic highs, and opening up to psychic or mind powers. In fact, if you are not careful they can become a serious digression preventing you from going even further on the spiritual path.

Pressing ahead further in meditative work, you will discover something even more profound and even radical. In short, you will completely change your identity from that of soul to what can be called for lack of a better term "Be-ness." And, the change to "Be-ness" is best effected through steady, constant, and more inner methods of approach. Some of these methods can include long term spiritually oriented counseling with a skilled spiritual teacher to help you integrate your many experiences during meditation practice in preparation for going even deeper. They can also include undergoing a formalized and intensive training in a religious system that emphasizes more the inner, or esoteric, side of the religion that is focused on a steady spiritualization of entire life. Or, you may undergo a long term spiritual discipline that includes a number of deep and more rigorous meditative and contemplative processes.

With these inner methods the approach changes from experiencing episodes that seem magical and mystical to those of steadily and consciously expanding your way of being through an inner change of not so much your mind, but of your *heart*. Too often those who engage in advanced meditation practices ignore this. They emphasize psychic and magical powers. Or, they emphasize what are really more powers of the mind that can enhance their sense of importance, and be employed for the sake of influencing others who will admire them as a personal and even spiritual success.

> The soul is often realized in silence, more than it is in dramatic experiences. Frequently, the soul reveals itself through a gentle whisper, a quiet nudge, and a sense of pervading calm, which hint that it's presence is near, much more than the fireworks and flash.

The result is one of personal power mixed in with seemingly spiritual powers, that are really more psychic in nature because the qualities of the soul are either lacking, or only cultivated and applied in the life at a superficial level. That is why it is often better and safer to simply cultivate a gentle heart, a reasonable grasp on reality, clear and consistent values, and a proportionate amount of humility over becoming absorbed in a whirlwind of tendencies amplified by expansions of consciousness, or psychic and mind powers that in truth only make one head-y with power. It is also helpful to understand the soul is often realized in silence, more than it is in dramatic experiences. Frequently, the soul reveals itself through a gentle whisper, a quiet nudge, and a sense of pervading calm, more than the fireworks and flash which often mask the still, small, voice of the soul wanting you to acknowledge its presence.

Meditation at this level then consists of practices that continually expand the heart, which in turn continually expand your identity. In a very real way meditation practice causes you to lose your sense of individuality. Though you remain a unique person with your own unique contribution, you no longer view yourself as an individual separate from the world, but as at-one with it. This sense of at-one-ment is not simply a platitude. It is a directive that now that you understand you are one with the world, you need to find ever deeper and more meaningful ways to serve it, since the world is essentially who you are.

From this point on you grow in your ability to consistently know yourself as energy. You realize that the same energy, which is expressing inself in the earth, sun, moon, and stars is likewise the same energy in you. That same energy is likewise found in minerals, plants, animals, and within your fellow human beings. As you wake up to this fact you continually ask yourself, "How can I experience the fullest measure of life and enjoy it fully without interfering in the rights of other living beings to do likewise?"

At another level these continual realizations help you

recognize what is eternal and important in your life. Thus, you learn to anchor your true sense of identity within the Eternal. Though everything in the world outside you can and will change, the more you identify yourself with the Eternal the more you realize that your essence, the essential *you* does not change. Your goals, intentions, identities, thoughts, feelings, actions, and body — all will change! But, the spark in you which is Eternal, which is at-one with all life, and in essence is energy that will not change. Outwardly, that spark will take on many shapes and forms. But inwardly, it will remain as it is, eternally resting contentedly within itself. Thus, liberation through your identification with the Eternal Spirit is produced.

Benefits, Exercise Six. Pause and reflect. How often have you considered yourself to be part of the whole around you? What would it mean in your life if you did? What would remain the same? What would change? Write your answers in a journal when you are finished.

It is not enough that you simply aspire to a spiritual life. You must live it on a daily basis. In this way you constantly expand spiritually as you refine and grow more into your spiritual being. A spiritual lifestyle is an evolving process, and to maintain a spiritual life requires a certain level of mastery. But, as you learn to polarize yourself and live from increasingly spiritual levels, you will likewise become increasingly creative and able to precipitate into the world at large new understandings of who we all really are and new approaches to help us all live more connected and at-one with each other. Meditation at this level is designed to facilitate this very process.

Transformational & Creative Benefits

TRANSFORMATIONAL BENEFITS

<u>Benefit Seven.</u> Facilitating the state of equilibrium at any one level by stabilizing the new vibration so an individual can embody and become the new level of identification.

In some texts a distinction is made between glimpses into the realm of the soul and illumination by the soul. Often these glimpses are mistaken as proof that one has reached the goal. This is similar to saying that occasional breaks in the cloud layer constitute a sunny day. Glimpses are important. They are meant to inspire you. They give you a hint as to possibilities that exist. And, glimpses come in many ways.

They may move through you like a sudden flash of insight. They may approach you through an act of loving kindness and concern from another. They may move you into the direction of being around fellow human beings who embody soul qualities. They may flood you with redemption and forgiveness for your fragile humanity and overbearing arrogance. Or, they may take you to heights of passion and ecstasy revealing a sweetness beyond your mundane life that you never imagined. Still, these are all glimpses. They are basically like flirtations or romantic dalliances with a lover. However, glimpses are not enough. They pierce the heart, but often do not change it fully. And it is loving hearts, not bleeding hearts, which are required as meditation leads you to live a fully loving and compassionate life.

Here then at this next phase meditation not only allows you to pierce through the clouds, but live above the clouds' domain. It is one thing to launch a plane into the air. It is another to keep it in the air so it can travel freely from place to place. Likewise, it is one thing to have moments of love, compassion and wise insight. And, it is another to live most of your life as a loving, compassionate, and wise human being.

This is what is meant by fancy words of equilibration, stabilizing the new vibration, and embodying the new identification. At the previous step you began to abstractly understand more about the soul and Spirit as energy. Here, you must not only expand your awareness of these dimensions, you must increasingly *walk your talk.* It is no longer what you say that is important. Rather, it is *what you do* and *who you are*. You inspire others *by being* that which you want them to be. Yes, there is value in ideas and information. Theories and stories regarding how to break a negative habit pattern or way of being are important. It's just at some time you need to *break the habit.* You need to be able to state that you have reached your goal, that your behavior has indeed changed. You want to see that *in fact* you are in a different place as a different person than when you started. Meditation can assist this, especially if you are not fooled by the mirages, or glimpses, that attempt to convince you that you have arrived, when you have not.

At this level meditation is also less oriented towards expansions of consciousness. These will continually occur. Rather, meditation is now a process of anchoring your understanding that you live in the eternal by revealing it to others primarily by sustaining yourself in its deep abiding peace. Because of this when you have truly reached this level you rarely, and ideally never, are disrupted mentally, emotionally, and physically by the transitory nature of your outer life.

> Suffering is after all, simply ignorance as to the true nature of the Universe as love. Aware of this suffering ceases. At the same time, out of your ability and desire to love others, you remain sensitive to the suffering around you.

This awareness so fills you with the reality of love in the Universe you are drenched in this love on a moment by moment basis. Despite all outer appearances of pain and suffering, the reason behind suffering is revealed to you. Suffering is after all, simply ignorance of our true nature as love. Aware of this love, suffering ceases. At the same time out of your ability and desire to love others, you remain sensitive to the suffering around you. You comprehend how ignorance continues to produce suffering in the world. Out of a need for compassion you do your best to relieve the world of this ignorance, and to awaken others regarding their true identities as spiritual beings. In this way the pain and trauma caused by an illusory separation from spiritual essence diminishes. The nature of Reality is increasingly revealed. That nature being primarily one of LOVE.

Benefit Exercise, Seven. Take some time to consider the following: "What would it mean to you if you were in fact, loved?" "If indeed, despite all outer appearances the Universe around you was a sea of compassion and love? And, that all appearance of suffering, were really manifestations of ignorance as to the existence of this love?" Think of the moments in your life when you felt you "glimpsed" this sense of love. Then ask yourself, "What would your life be like and how would you be if no matter what happened to you in life, this presence of love, always infused you, and surrounded you?" After reflecting for some minutes, affirm to yourself here and now, "I am One with All. All is Love. This is my only security. This is my only identity." Stay with this affirmation and as you do so, reflect how it feels to rest within this statement.

CREATIVE BENEFITS

<u>Benefit Eight.</u> Allowing for the insights which help produce the means to be creative at whatever new level of identification one has reached.

If applied, your practice of meditation so far has been a rich one. After having transformed yourself into a new level of being, you strive to help others benefit from it through a radiation of your new Being as a being of love, and through creative endeavors that reflect this. After years of training and discipline your life becomes an art form. You express in a spontaneous and alive manner because the skills of learning how to be creative as a loving and compassionate human being have become second nature. They drop below the "threshold of consciousness." You no longer need to pay attention to them. They are part of your being as new and natural habits — as effortless to master as the breath in your body, and the beat of your heart.

> Ultimately, meditation lets you be creative from an expanded and loving point of identification with everything around you. Remember the fruitful benefits you garnish from meditation cannot be kept to yourself. They must be shared.

By this time you have begun to understand that the real benefit of meditation practice goes beyond means of relaxing and controlling the body, working more effectively with your emotions, observing your thoughts and improving concentration, and so forth. Ultimately, meditation lets you be creative from an expanded and loving point of identification with everything and everyone around you. Remember the fruitful benefits you garnish from meditation cannot be kept to yourself. They must be shared. Like seeds they need to be spread around encouraging other saplings to grow. Meditation practice will give you many insights regarding how to do this. Ideally, these insights have a purpose. Spiritually, the best purpose is increased awareness how others are best served by your unique talents and the spiritual presence you have learned to become.

From this stage forward *all of life becomes a meditation.* Life evolves into the continued opportunity for spiritually inspired creative living! At the highest form, meditation allows you to continually tap into the Source of life, with its powerful capacity to energize and renew you. When every moment of your day becomes an opportunity for expansion of your awareness, when you can learn to breathe into your life a constant recognition of yourself as Spirit, life takes on a new texture that is rich, vibrant, and exquisite. The pulsating energy of the sun, the radiant glory of the stars, the constant reminder via each and every breath you take that you are both breathing, and being breathed by Spirit — all these allow you to know that even within the darkest moments of despair and heartache, beauty and love *is* at the core of all existence. For every disappointment is really an invitation to open up and expand your awareness as to the essence of yourself as Spirit. And, from this essence you then can create and re-create your life as never before so that it resonates more deeply with the Spirit you are that relates to others through compassion and love.

Creation in a sense is not an activity then, but a way of Being. Like a spider weaving a thread from within its substance, you weave the threads of reality in your life connecting each strand of it with those around you. Finally, the web of life is so inter-related you never forget you are really ONE common humanity. Together we all live in this beautiful, precious, and fragile place we call Earth, as well as in a vast and glorious Cosmos. Standing within this, meditation reaches its peak and dissolves. It has done its work; its gifts are now yours.

Benefits, Exercise Eight. Pause again for the final time. Close your eyes and sit quietly. Focus on your breath. As you breathe in and out consider that with each breath you breathe in, you expand your identity with the whole, and with each breath you breathe out you contribute something greater to the whole. Do this exercise for a minimum of five minutes. With each breath in and out, expand your sense of who you are and what you can contribute. As you conclude the exercise, allow a sense of stillness to come into your heart. Rest quietly within this, and when at last you are ready, open your eyes.

Building Blocks for Meditation

Now that you have a clearer understanding of the benefits of meditation it is time to get down to the basics of learning how to meditate. To effectively meditate certain fundamentals must be understood and mastered. These involve disciplines related to the body, the emotions, and the mind. Some of these disciplines have already been mentioned in brief. Here a few more details will be given to give you a clearer understanding.

Focusing on these basics related to the body, emotions, and the mind is important. Then your attempts to meditate you will not become distracted by the needs of your body (aches, pains, hunger, sensations), or your physical needs (including for food, clothing, shelter). Nor will your emotional needs and impulses dominate your meditation time in the way of emotional desires, excitements, depressions, and irritations. And, if your mental thoughts are unruly, scattered, harsh, and mundane, exalted meditative states will not be reached if you only stay focused on your mental worries. That is why the following basic meditation practices are necessary to help you discipline your physical, emotional, and mental bodies so you can subdue them and lift your attention elsewhere. These basic disciplines in short are known as relaxation, visualization, and concentration.

RELAXATION

Most people are familiar with the aspect of meditation practice known as relaxation. It has become popularized in the general marketplace, and is generally accepted for its health producing effects. Relaxation is a tool which focuses upon the physical body. It uses forms of light hypnosis and biofeedback to teach you to work with the muscular system and regulatory functions of the body so they can come under your conscious control. The primary technique of relaxation usually involves moving slowly through the body progressively relaxing the various muscle groups. More advanced relaxation practices go even further and teach you how to control bodily functions such as your heart beat and breathing to deepen the overall relaxation response. In this respect relaxation is related to the Eastern discipline known as Hatha Yoga, which also works to help you gain conscious control over your physical instrument.

In general, relaxation techniques have become popular under the guise of stress management. When you do not honor the cycles of activity and rest in your life, you create imbalances that impact you negatively through stress. By learning to relax you help restore this balance. Also, by practicing relaxation you achieve many different health effects. In paying attention to the way in which you tense needlessly your muscles, you become conscious of how you hold stress in your body. By learning to regulate your breathing and heart rate, you keep the body in balance and full of more vitality. For this reason the Western reductionistic medical model accepts relaxation techniques the most because it's effects can be measured, studied, and observed. Relaxation has also become the most popular building block to meditation practice because its effects are so immediate.

VISUALIZATION

Everyone possesses the capacity to see pictures with their imaginations, and for some this picture making faculty is highly developed. The pictures they create are filled with textures, brilliant colors, varying hues, depth, and dimension. For others, the ability to conjure up pictures in their mind's eye is a difficult labor. Any pictures generated tend to be flat, colorless, and difficult to bring into focus. For this reason, they either ignore the process of visualization or have to approach it by learning to see simple pictures first, like a circle with a dot at the center, adding complexity later.

> Visualization becomes important in meditation in two ways. First, as a useful tool for working ith emotions. Second, as part of the creative meditation process.

Visualization becomes an important ingredient in meditation in two ways. First, visualizations are useful in working with emotional issues. As mentioned before visualizations are frequently used to help various emotional states resolve in harmonious ways such as when you view your emotions as a calm pool of water. You can also imagine the resolution of various emotional issues by taking yourself on imaginary journeys to different places that may bring about an emotional state of feeling tranquil, harmonious, and at peace. Other visualizations that are emotionally based will have you travel to imaginary worlds where you undergo adventures, talk to invisible people, find ways to relax, or in general just escape from the realm you are in.

Though these kind of visualizations are useful, it is important to understand that they primarily work on an emotional level. What they are really doing is engaging your creative imagination primarily for entertainment or emotional healing. Especially if you are natural storyteller, fictional writer, artist, or actor you are likely to have the visual faculty strongly developed. Visualization practices will be not only easy for you, they will appeal to you. You will also be able to stimulate this visual component in others.

The only dilemma when visualizations are linked to meditation and spiritual practice is that if the mental faculties are not well developed then spiritual progress can actually be hindered as you trip off continually into fantasy worlds without attempting to really analyze the deeper validity of any visual adventures you are having. For example, are you really in touch with beings from another realm or just your own imagination? Are those beings really saying anything truly useful and insightful that can't just be found in any basic psychology or even spirituality course? Is what they are saying really valid or are you just succumbing to glamour and flights of fancy, especially if these visual encounters are feeding your sense of importance and therefore your own ego?

Of course if you are too emotionally based chances are you won't even want to consider the above questions because you will be overly attached to your imaginary journeys, especially if they reinforce that you have a unique or special place in the world because of what these visualizations are revealing to you. And, that is precisely the problem. If you are special and the teaching you are attached to is from such an exalted level in your mind it can't even be questioned, then the truth is you are not developing your higher mental and spiritual capabilities. Why? Because at the mental stage of development everything is open to being questioned. And, at the spiritual stage of development visual and mental images and journeys become increasingly irrelevant.

The second form of visualization is more sophisticated then just going on imaginary journeys because it is more mentally based. Here visualization becomes part of the creative meditation process, which will be spoken about at more length later. In creative meditation the goal is to condition your mind, brain, and nervous response mechanism along certain lines so that certain effects can be produced in your life. When confronted with various situations you are then better able to handle them according to how you have pre-programmed them. Many athletes actively work in this way as they frequently picture an event, like winning a gold medal in their minds. By repeatedly imagining running a race or skiing down a hill, they heighten the probability of success when participating in the actual event because they have already mentally and emotionally gone through it so many times.

Visualizations can also be used therapeutically at this level especially in regards to healing past traumatic events. Even though a painful situation may have happened years ago it is stored as a memory in the brain that can be triggered and repeated mentally over and over again. By going back in time and re-imagining or re-visualizing the event in a more positive light the reactivity and pain around the event can be minimized. Also, insights for how to give spiritual meaning to the event, or regarding how else the event could have been handled, can arise.

For example if you were robbed in the past at gunpoint, you might imagine that you saw the robbers and their harmful intentions sooner and were able to act in a more positive and preventive way. When working with visualizations in this way the goal is not to deny the reality of your past, but to change the emotional and mental charge related to it. The more vivid these visualizations, the more effectively these triggers can be reconditioned, and you can be freed from old habit patterns that hinder your present functioning in life.

Finally, visualizations can go beyond the mind and be used as very specific spiritual tools. The elaborate symbols found in many religious systems are examples of this. These symbols are pregnant with meaning. Often each color, line, and image is selected and placed in certain ways for specific reasons. The idea is to simultaneously see the image, reflect on its meaning, and embody its meaning into your way of being in your everyday life. As these types of visualizations are very complex they are often rarely used by many people. But, they are highly rewarding and insightful when serious spiritual students do undergo them.

CONCENTRATION

Concentration is the primary tool for working with the mind, as it helps you focus your attention on a particular thought for a prolonged period of time. The mind no longer engages in flights of fancy or skips from one stage to the next. Rather, the mind is quieted and controlled. It is no longer known as the "monkey mind" swinging from thought to thought and chattering endlessly out of control. Instead, the mind is able to pay attention to the task before it, whether it is emotionally or physically rewarding to do so. For many people, concentration practices can seem tedious and even dull. Finding ways to motivate yourself to practice concentration exercises can be difficult, therefore, if you don't fully understand the rewards.

One of the major rewards is that of discovering that the

more you can command your mind to pay attention, the more mind control you will have. You will also become increasingly aware of the content of your thought life and discover how much of it may stem from being conditioned to think in ways that no longer serve you. Aware of this you can shed limiting beliefs and learn to consciously and carefully select thoughts that are more life enhancing at will. And, you will become less mentally and emotionally reactive as you understand more the mental triggers, or belief systems, that lead you to think certain thoughts and respond in certain ways.

When you begin to comprehend the importance of mental mastery it is easier to value concentration and understand why it is so essential to real meditation work. Since real meditation requires the ability to still the mind and focus it at will, it becomes obvious that meditation in the truest sense cannot occur without concentration as foundational work. Using music as a metaphor concentration is equivalent to the stage of having to learn the basic notes by spending hours a day simply playing scales. In time the fundamentals of learning the notes ends and your ability to play beautiful music the way you want to emerges. In a similar way meditation is not possible without learning the notes and practicing the scales of mastering the work of concentrating your thoughts and calming them at will.

If you feel discouraged about your ability to learn concentration exercises remember everyone to some degree has participated in concentration whether formally trained or not. For example, whenever you attempt to organize your thoughts on a piece of paper you are beginning to concentrate your thoughts. Likewise, in studying a book, reviewing a series of information, skiing down a hill, driving a car, or administrating a task concentration is occurring. Naturally, the more routine any task becomes, the less you have to concentrate and focus on it and the more you enter into a mindless state often known as *flow*. It is so natural to you, it just is. But, before you can reach flow, before you can reach higher states of meditation, concentration is needed. Though you may not desire it, it is good to see how a concentrated mind is actually a disciplined mind, that allows you to accomplish what you want because you are no longer distracted or subjected to seemingly uncontrollable urges or thoughts that lead you in a direction that is not truly serving your best interests.

Now that we have covered the basics to meditation, let's go on to some of the other building blocks for meditation that include a better understanding of meditation and its related element known as contemplation.

MEDITATION

Going back to the Webster's definition of meditation mentioned earlier in this book meditation was said to have the synonym of pondering. Pondering involves concentration, but differs from it. Pondering implies an attempt to enter into the realm of meaning. It contains within it an attempt to arrive at some sort of insight or understanding. And, it is often driven by the need to ask questions in order to find their solutions. A few examples clearly illustrate the difference. You may be concentrating when driving a car, but not view driving as a meaningful activity. Or, you may concentrate on not falling as you ski down a hill, but there may be no meaning or significant importance to it since you may just want to have a good time and enjoy the view. Looked at a different way if you are trying to ski down a hill to win an Olympic event then a great deal of meaning might be attached going beyond simply concentration at this point.

Whenever meaning enters into the picture you are entering more the domain of meditation, since now you are attempting to ponder or understand something or someone. That is why many people first enter into real meditation work as a means for finding solutions to significantly pressing problems. At this level meditation attempts to understand cause and effect — if I do this, it leads to that. In many ways there is a scientific aspect to meditation as meditation is used to logically reason something out to arrive at certain understandings and solutions. However, meditation goes beyond the reasoning process and helps you tap into direct knowing through intuition.

Many people think they understand what the intuition is, yet in many cases the word is used incorrectly. For example, intuition is much more than a gut reaction. These gut reactions are actually just instinctual responses based upon your digested and prior conditioning of understanding how to respond in certain events. And, intuition in the truest sense is much more than a psychic impression (like knowing someone is about to call on the phone who then does). The word intuition as it is used in this book is more akin to new ideas, a-ha's, insights, or original thoughts that have *never been considered before*. Advanced meditators frequently tap into the realm of intuition where original ideas and solutions can be found. In fact the mysterious realm from which intuitions come are said to not even reside within the brain and body, though they penetrate the brain at some point.

The realm of the intuition resides instead in the realm of consciousness. This realm has been given many names in spiritual traditions. Hindus or Buddhists may refer to it as the realm of universal mind. And, Jews, Christians, and Muslims have sometimes called it the "raincloud of knowable things." Through meditation these intuitions are accessed so that solutions to problems and inquiries come to you. Then, to assess the accuracy of your intuitions, you may be guided to outside sources like books, people, scientific methodology, to confirm them. This confirmation process is important to help you avoid the distortion of intuitive impressions that are really more like psychic hunches that often are inaccurate.

The more you develop the intuition the more you will be able to answer questions and find solutions in your life seemingly without the apparent help of outside aid. You will then go beyond the scientific reasoning process. Though scientific methods do engage some cause and effect pondering, these methods are based on known premises and substantiated by known data. (I know this makes this happen, so it stands to reason that this also makes this happen, since this is similar to that). Intuitive knowing is different. Here you do not start with a hypothesis or preconceived notions you are attempting to prove or disprove. Instead, you begin with a seed-thought, usually posed as a question, and then arrive at answers via the light of the intuition. Or, you simply quiet the mind and orient it in a certain direction in order to gain insights and answers.

As you get those insights and answers it is important to see that an intuitive response is not simply guess work involving 50-50 odds. As mentioned these are more likely psychic impressions that exist at the emotional level and reflect that you have not developed your mental body enough. Remember, intuition is above the realm of the mind, not below it hanging about in emotional realms. That is why true intuitions are much more exact. And, it is why intuitive impressions are almost always corroborated later as being based in fact within our time/ space world.

Because meditation often requires a great deal of thought, it is natural that a meditative mind becomes an inquiring mind. In short, the more you meditate the more profound and deep your questions and insights will become. That is why meditation leads you into a depth of understanding. Life becomes pregnant with meaning. Life has significance. Life becomes increasingly precious and valuable. As you understand this you naturally tend to relate to life more holistically. This in turn alters your identification leading to greater and greater experiences of at-one-ment with the whole. And, as you meditate more you will mature in both wisdom and compassion, which leads to the last building block to consider — contemplation.

> In meditation the intuitive faculty of the mind is engaged to help you find meaningful solutions to profound questions.
> In contemplation, you enter the realm of holiness.
> You align and attune yourself to the Divine itself.

CONTEMPLATION

On the surface, contemplation seems synonymous with meditation. Just as the distinctions between concentration and meditation are often confused in people's minds, contemplation and meditation are often blurred. Even in Webster's dictionary contemplation is defined as "to meditate upon." What then is the difference between the two stages of practice? It is helpful to look at the etymology of the two words, “con” and “template.” Simply put, the word "con" refers to the word with. It also brings in the notion of "keeping something in view." The word template relates to something which can reflect or copy something else. As mentioned, meditation involves meaning at some level. But, contemplation goes beyond simply reflection. Rather, it makes of the mind itself a template — something that is clear, receptive, and reflective of spiritual realms.

Meditation practice at this level involves keeping the mind stuff (called “chitta” in Eastern traditions) still for long durations of time. The mind is not asleep, however. It is not inactive. It is simply reflective. This does not mean it is reflective in the vein of thinking about something. That is known as meditation. In contemplation the mind is not thinking at all. It is put into a holding pattern. Yet, it is not just an empty sponge absorbing anything and everything. Contemplation is not a state of sleep. It does not mean you go into a trance. You are not trying to go somewhere else or just sitting there being quiet. Rather, you are both quieting the mind, while actively aligning and orienting it along certain lines of spiritual intent or light, so that you can receive subtle impressions from the spiritual realms that you are oriented to. In short, a contemplative mind is an aligned mind — aligned to that which it wants to reflect.

As the contemplative mind is quiet and focused certain experiences may arise including those of both experiencing light, or those of entering into a deep void pregnant with darkness. But, even here you are not in a trance. You are in a space of awareness that has taken you in a very sacred space. To help you understand notice that the word contemplation contains the word temple. A temple is defined as "an edifice dedicated to the worship of deity." This reinforces the idea that contemplation involves the ability to stand receptive to Deity, even receptive to the Deity you are!

In contemplation then you enter the realm of holiness. You align and attune yourself to the Divine itself. You enter into a state of reverence. This differs from an emotional state of awe. It is more akin to being caught up and absorbed into the Divine. In many ways it becoming absorbed into the purest state of love. And, that love moves the mind beyond itself into a state of rapture where it is fixated into place for long periods of time without becoming fatigued, distracted, or debilitated in any way. There in this state you not only enter bliss, you go beyond it into the “peace that passeth all understanding,” which is a major fruit of spiritual experience.

Other Types of Meditation Practice

Thus far five building blocks to meditation have been mentioned: relaxation, visualization, concentration, meditation, and contemplation. To reach the highest levels of meditation practice, these five stages are important to develop. In this chapter four additional types of meditation will be mentioned: creative meditation, mind over matter, devotion, worship and prayer. Not all of these lead to the ultimate goal of meditation practice — recognition of and at-one-ment with the Divine. In fact, creative meditation and mind over matter trainings in particular can be applied from a purely egotistical and selfish level with no spiritual motivation or realization involved.

As for devotion and worship these do have a spiritual motivation, yet they approach divinity in primarily a dualistic way. That is they act as if Deity is separate from you, not a part of you. For this reason they do not always lead to an experience of at-one-ment with the Divine. Finally, we have prayer. Depending on how prayer is used it can operate at many different levels. From a selfish level prayer can simply be a way to attempt to expunge yourself of guilt for misdeeds, or to trick and win favors from the Divine in order to make your wishes come true. Prayer can even be used to wish ill or harm on other people. Clearly, when prayer is used in these ways it does little to affirm or help you penetrate into a spiritual state.

On another level prayer can help you establish a meaningful connection with the Divine, though again there is a dualistic aspect to prayer (I am here, Deity is over there.) Still, at the highest level prayer may actually be similar to meditation or even contemplation, if you use prayer to gain insight or enter into a receptive silence to hear the Divine within you. Let's review these forms of meditation practice more in depth.

CREATIVE MEDITATION

Creative meditation is a particular method of meditation that partakes of the qualities of concentration, visualization, and meditation, but does not necessarily bring in the deeper levels of contemplation. In this technique the mind is intent upon manifesting something upon the physical plane. This could be anything such as a new car, a business, a mate, a child, a life long ambition fulfilled. In popular times creative meditation is now known under a different name, the law of attraction.

When looked at carefully it is easy to see that the technical steps of creative meditation can be either selfishly or selflessly employed. The determining factor is motivation.

When looked at carefully it is easy to see that the technical steps of creative meditation can be either selfishly or selflessly employed. The determining factor is motivation, which is also something I addressed at some length in my *Beyond the Secret: Spiritual Power and the Law of Attraction* book. There I attempted to reveal the difference between the egotistical and spiritual uses of creative meditation or the law of attraction processes. For example, if you use your mind powers to satisfy only personal cravings, then the spiritual element is negated. After all getting a new car may have nothing to do with a spiritual need for it. Also, the methods employed to get the new car may be immoral or even illegal. I spoke about this shadow side of the law of attraction that includes the "evil wish," the "downfall wish," and more in my *Beyond the Secret: Spiritual Power and the Law of Attraction* book.

When creative meditation is used on a more spiritual level it is primarily a means of discovering your spiritual calling by using creative meditation techniques to help you create a service activity that illumines and uplifts not only yourself, but others. Though the methods used will be technically the same as those employed to get a new car, the spiritual use is oriented towards helping other people through the use of your creative powers beyond just yourself.

For this reason, creative meditation has some times been divided into two types known in older religious texts as white, gray, and black magic. The use of the word magic in these older texts implies that in creative meditation some sort of supernatural element is involved in the process. This is somewhat unfortunate because there is nothing supernatural about creative meditation. It is simply a technical process employing the natural laws of the mind. Like anything, however, it only seems magical to those who do not understand it.

The words white and black in our modern era are also unfortunate and can even seem pejorative. Still, their use is intended to help you understand the motive underlying the creative meditation process. White magic uses the creative powers of the mind to heal, uplift, and spiritualize yourself and others. Black magic uses these powers to destroy, rob, and degrade others in your attempts to gratify your desires. Gray magic involves a mixture of both since your motives are also mixed. Though you hope others will benefit from the fruits of your creative labor, you are also concerned that you benefit in the process, and often you hope that you benefit somewhat more than those around you. Determining the underlying motivation in the creative process is difficult. Therefore, using the words white and black magic can be deceptive. In my *Beyond the Secret: Spiritual Power and the Law of Attraction* book I avoided these terms, preferring to use the words spiritual versus egotistical, since that is what is really implied here.

Since the methods for creative meditation are the same regardless of the motive, learning to perceive the motive in yourself and others takes an act of clear spiritual perception to discern it. This is especially the case if your own, or someone else's motives are mixed. In helping to ensure that the motives tend to be more spiritual a strong sense of ethics needs to be cultivated through spiritual work. That is why in my *Beyond the Secret: Spiritual Power and the Law of Attraction* book I laid the foundation first for orienting towards spirit, negating the ego, and attracting the soul so you have a more spiritual approach.

MIND OVER MATTER

Another form of meditation practice attempts to use the powers of the mind to control and manipulate mental, emotional, and physical substance. Some of this has already been alluded to when covering the benefits of meditation in these three areas. Attempts to use the mind to manipulate matter are also seen in various psychic powers real or imagined. Here claims are made to be able to read the minds of others, or to even manipulate items without physically contacting them. The character of Yoda in the *Star Wars* trilogy demonstrates an example of this ability when he states he uses "the Force" to move a large space ship out of the mud.

In real life numerous claims are made of various psychics and yogis who manifest ash and rings out of nowhere, or who bend spoons, tip tables, and so forth. There are even events where popular speakers and motivational teachers attempt to get participants to walk over hot coals, or withstand difficult situations by attempting to will their thoughts, emotions, and bodies to overcome whatever obstacles are in front of them. Then there are the various so called "faith healings" that claim to heal the physical body through the power of the mind alone. On the milder side there is the use of mind over matter as simply a means of disciplining your thoughts and mobilizing your will so that you can effectively follow through on your intentions.

What is really going on in these various mind over matter techniques is up for debate. Some people view these mind powers as unreal and see their so called use as simply examples of how people can succumb to fanciful and even preposterous notions. Others state that these seemingly fantastical episodes (like Moses parting the Red Sea or Jesus walking on water) are meant to be allegorical or metaphorical in nature. In other words, they are not meant to be taken seriously as fact. So in the examples of Moses and Jesus the water stands for the emotional body. Therefore, what Moses and Jesus were really doing was working with the emotional bodies of themselves and others effectively. They were symbolic, not real events.

Then there are those who are open to the possibility of these powers existing, but they like to maintain a certain amount of healthy skepticism until they can prove through experience that there is a factual and scientific basis to mind over matter claims. There are also people who say their life experiences have proven the validity of mind over matter techniques, so they don't need scientific confirmation.

Regardless of how real these powers are, it should be

noted they are primarily mind powers, and are by no means spiritual ones. In our modern day technological world we can do many things that just a few short years ago would have seemed miraculous. Still, discovering and inventing something that allows us to control matter or the environment better is no sign that a spiritual motivation or intention is behind the discovery. The desire for money and power may just have well been the impulse.

Regardless of how real these powers are, it should be noted they are primarily mind powers, and are by no means spiritual ones. And, spiritual powers need not even be employed to make them work. One only needs a powerfully concentrated mind, energized by a dynamic will.

For this reason it is important to understand that so called psychic or mind powers may also have no real spiritual connection. And, spiritual powers may not even be employed to make them work. All that is needed is a powerfully concentrated mind, energized by a dynamic will, with some level of visual acuity to put these techniques into motion. When disconnected from the heart the employment of these techniques can even lead to disaster.

The episode of James Ray, the law of attraction guru, sitting passively by as people died in his sweat lodge is a sign of this. Though his teachings were focused on helping his followers master their minds, it did not necessarily help him or them stay open to their hearts, or they would have been sensitive and not indifferent to people dying around them. And, this lack of heart that often happens when mind over matter techniques are employed is one reason criminal charges were pressed against

James Ray to remind him and us that heart is the more important than powers exerted by the mind alone.

Remember spiritual powers are higher than mind powers. They employ the ability to love, heal, unify, uplift, and be at-one with the Divine. Ironically, spiritual powers are not even viewed as very powerful, or even as important or "spiritual" as mind powers. That is because the spiritual capacity to heal someone's heart may not seem as dramatic as a mind power of getting that person to walk on hot coals. Yet, spiritual powers are more powerful in the long run. You may cross over the hot coals and remain just as emotionally insensitive as you were before you started over them. In fact, your emotional insensitivity may have helped you cross them with ease. Still, that same emotional insensitivity may also be turning you into an egotistical and abusive individual who manipulates others for your own personal gain. For this reason mind over matter techniques are seen as possible digressions from the spiritual path because too often they lead to the love of power, and not enough to the healing and compassionate power of love.

DEVOTION

In devotion, worship, and prayer we have aspects of meditation practice that are often thought to be the same as meditation, but may or may not be similar. Devotion implies a certain degree of loyal adherence to someone or something. When you devote yourself you give of your entire being (mind, body, and soul) to the welfare of whatever or whoever is the object of your devotion. Devotion involves a concentrated mind fueled by the passion and intensity of your emotional nature in relation to a particular object, person or goal. Though emotions are always involved to some degree in the practice of devotion, they can if properly employed help lift you into some exalted spiritual realms.

But, on the lower levels devotion can result in problematic attachments which are obsessive, compulsive, and illusory. They can also come from fear, insecurity, and neediness resulting frequently from a fear of losing that which you are attached to. And, blind devotion can even be led by naive, foolish, indiscriminative, and unbalanced emotionalism. Here you are devoted not because of your steadfast love, but because you are impelled by compulsive needs. When these needs are not met, devotion rapidly sours, leaving anger and bitterness in its wake.

At the highest level, devotion helps you reach heights of spiritual awareness. When positively directed devotion is a beautiful thing to behold. The best of marriages or friendships rely on devotion to help keep the bond of love intact when adverse times might strain or break the relationship altogether. When applied to spirituality devotion to a spiritual teacher or truth can inspire you to improve your life and help you fashion your life according to spiritual ideals. Devotion can also give you the necessary resilience you need to improve and refine your life despite resistance and adversity. And, devotion aids you in penetrating into life's deeper meaning. To participate in meditation, afterall, requires a loyal adherence of the mind towards understanding some aspect of truth on a deeper level.

At its best devotion gives your emotional body the fuel to persist, to believe, to strive forward in your spiritual development. You move from ideal to ideal, yearning to perfect your experience of the transcendent. Devotion is necessary then to some degree when pursuing a spiritual path, especially when it sustains your momentum to enter into deeper levels of spiritual life, and does not sidetrack you into deluded emotional reactions. These deluded reactions happen when the emotional body is employed more than the mental body. Then the mind is not utilized to discriminate or think clearly. The sticky glue properties of your emotional devotion simply make you addicted and attached to the object of your devotion. You even fail to consider whether such devotion is wise in the first place, which is one reason people succumb to being devoted to "spiritual" teachers who are really just charismatic and use that charisma to manipulate followers into giving them favors in the way of financial and sexual compensation. They may even insist on followers giving up their lives just to protect the leaders from facing the delusions and addictions of their own egos.

> At its best devotion gives your emotional body
> the fuel to persist, to believe, to strive forward
> in your spiritual development.

Whether your devotion is quiet or intense, it may endure for a long period of time, or burn out quickly. It all depends on your expectations of what you hope to receive in return from that which you are devoted to. In conclusion, it should be noted that devotion is primarily a dualistic spiritual approach. Deity is not viewed as in you it is seen as outside of you. The rate at which devotion burns away depends upon the ending of dualistic perceptions. If you finally get what is desired over there, it becomes a part of you. Thus, there is no need to be devoted anymore. Example: Someone rarely feels devoted to an idea which they have not only assimilated, but have now outgrown. Still devotion is an important part of spiritual practice. In fact, it can even help you reach the heights of meditation practice simply because you become devoted to meditation itself.

WORSHIP

Worship is a heightened form of devotion and is also dualistic. Unlike prayer it adds the additional element of placing something above you, while you are beneath it in stature. There is nothing wrong with this. Some things in life truly are above you and for this reason deserve reverence and respect. Often in the experience of the divine you are called upon to worship it. This is based on a feeling of awe and an appreciation for the powerful forces immanent in that which is revered. Worship can bring out marvelous qualities of humility. When you truly see and respect that which is above you, you have a better sense of proportion regarding your actual capacities and can be inspired to strive towards that which represents your future development. When worship is motivated out of fear, however, it loses some of the spiritual element. With fear at the core you are incapable of seeing that which you worship clearly. Instead, you see a fantasy that you invest with certain powers, expectations, and qualities which may be mostly an illusion.

Often the fear is mixed with anxiety and even disdain. That is why at times a certain degree of discomfort occurs when being around the worshipped object. The powerful forces are experienced, but they are not seen as beneficent in nature. Instead, they are seen as controlling and dominating forces that must be obeyed for the sake of survival. If one could do without these forces, one believes they would be all the better. But, since this cannot occur, the powerful force must be appeased somehow, and worship becomes the main method of doing so. In this example, worship has little to do with spirituality though on the surface you may believe it does.

Though worship aids the meditation process when rightly employed, it is not akin to meditation. The dynamic of worship is more an upward pouring out of feeling, than a focused intention to gain insight. On the lower level, worship detracts from the ability to meditate because of its failure to make use of the mind. On the higher level, worship brings balance to the individual adding vital qualities of humility and perspective to what may be too arid or even ambitious (from an egotistical level) of a meditative approach.

PRAYER

Prayer is another dualistic approach to spiritual practice. As mentioned earlier depending on how it is employed it can be synonymous with meditation. If you pray as a means to silently commune with your inner self to receive guidance or an answer to a pressing need or question, then you have entered into the domain of meditation, and are simply calling it by a different name. You are basically in a listening stage where you must be focused, silent, and receptive to the answer.

When prayer is more petitionary in nature, though valuable, it loses the meditative flavor. "I am in pain, help me out of it." "I need money, please send some my way." "My spouse is a difficult person, help me to have the patience to deal with him." "My best friend is ailing, use your power and wisdom to help him recover." In these examples different degrees of sincere and selfish motivation are present. Some of the demands are altruistic. Others are little more than an excuse to get out of the responsibility of living a mature life.

Like anything, prayer can be an art form. Petitionary prayer used in a selfless manner can be useful in your spiritual development. It is a means of conversing with divinity, not only listening to it. It is also a means of sending your loving thoughts towards others. Caution is advised, however, if petitionary prayer sets up a dynamic where you become solely a lost and dependent person in need of the services of some powerful divine intervention. Meditation remember teaches you that you have access to answers that can help you in life if you will only take the time to develop qualities of spiritual maturity and responsibility. When prayer is used too passively it erodes this inner awareness. True prayer goes beyond merely feeling helpless and passive in the face of the Divine. Instead, it combines courage, determination, and wisdom so that your difficulties can move beyond seeking out a temporary rescue from the Divine into learning how to permanently changing your life for the better.

At a higher turn of the spiral if prayer is used in a more spiritual way, the ideal state of mind is one of sincere love and friendship in relation to that to which you are praying to. When you solicit help of some kind, it is best done with a trusting and loving heart. This lifts it into more of an equal relationship, yet retains some of the needed humility. "I come to you as one who loves you, trusts you, and knows that you are capable of fulfilling my needs. As a friend I invite you to assist me. In return, as always, I would be most grateful. If you are unable to fulfill my need, then as your friend, I would still be grateful, and would even understand and accept the basis for your decisions." In this way prayer elicits from you the highest level of spiritual maturity.

Mediation Aids

For meditation to exist certain components must be in operation. These components are not methods of meditation, but rather supplements to it. They either influence the direction meditation takes, amplify the process, or provide the focus for meditative work. For this reason they are considered aids to the meditative process. And, they are distinct from props used in meditation work. Props are physical objects that may be used like special pillows, mats, and chairs. Props also include music, rosary beads, and sacred items of worship. The aids referred to here are mental tools. They include invocation, evocation, affirmations, mantras, and meditation entered into with or without a seed thought.

INVOCATION & EVOCATION

Invocation and its counterpart evocation are essential parts of the meditative process. The word invoke means to call down. The word evoke relates to calling something forth. When the mind is focused in meditation, invocation acts like a focused thread of intention between the higher and lower minds. This thread connects you to spiritual realms and insights within a particular arena. In a sense the thread acts as an antenna which helps you tune into specific frequencies through your meditation alignment to them. Invocation therefore is really more like a function, or adjunct, to facilitate meditation. For example, a cup serves the function of assisting you in the activity of drinking. Likewise, invocation serves the function of aiding you in the activity of meditation.

The more conscious and exact you are in using invocative processes the more potent the insights and illuminations you will be able to receive in meditation. For invocation to work you must be able to hold your meditation alignment steady until an answer comes from spiritual realms along the lines of your specified intent. This means you must learn how to keep the static out of your meditation alignment. This static includes external physical noise as well as internal emotional and mental noise. For example, let's say you set up your meditation alignment with the intent to invoke insights regarding how to be more loving along certain lines in your life. However, during your meditation if all you hear is the clock ticking, or mainly focus on your irritation with someone, or keep going back to your to-do list throughout the day, you are not really holding your meditation alignment. Static is interfering and your meditation will likely be wasted since little to no insight on how to be more loving emerges.

> Invocation is more a bringing down energies from the intangible hidden world of forces, so they can become more tangible. Evocation is a drawing out of potentials and possibilities in a person or thing, so they can become more self-evident, strengthened, and encouraged.

With invocation comes evocation. The only difference between the two words is the realm of application. In invocation you are seeking to call forth something from the inner intangible worlds. In evocation, you are directed to the outer world of objectivity. Invocation is more a "bringing down" from the intangible hidden world of forces, so they can become more tangible. Evocation is a "drawing out" of potentials and possibilities in a person or thing, so they can become more self-evident, strengthened, and encouraged. You invoke a solution to your problem via the realm of intuition. You evoke a greater sense of love and compassion from your spouse who has just been hostile to you. Finally, in invocation you are the passive receiver and are acted upon by another force. While in evocation you are the dynamic transmitter acting upon another in the hopes of producing a certain effect.

Invocation and evocation also go hand in hand. One cannot exist without the other. When a new insight is invoked concerning how you may change your life for the better, mental, emotional, and physical patterns are evoked in relation to this. For example: An illumination comes by way of invocation regarding a need to change to a more suitable type of work. As the idea of changing work impacts you mental thoughts surface as to what you now must practically do. As you think about changing work emotional excitement, or anxieties and fears may arise. So might physical reactions such as sweat and a more rapid heartbeat. These are all the results of the evocative process. Aware of this you can invoke a way to manage your reactions more effectively. As these new insights come, additional mental, emotional, and physical responses that enable you to respond more constructively to the situation may be evoked.

SEED THOUGHTS

A seed-thought is a word or phrase which you use during the process of meditation and contemplation. There are as many seed-thoughts as there are words used by the human family. The purpose in using a word as a seed-thought is to understand more deeply its meaning and significance. Take the word love for example. In everyday communication you may use the word love in a number of ways. "I love chocolate." "I love my children." "Don't you just love the way he throws the ball?" "All the world needs is love." "I love her so much I can't stand it."

In each of these phrases the word love never changes. But, the meaning of love and the significance the word love carries, is very different. When you say you love chocolate, do you mean it in the same way as when you say you love your children? Is the love of chocolate as significant as the love for a fellow human? When you begin to think about the answers to these questions, you move into the realm of meditation. A seed thought is therefore a word or statement that you use in meditation to gain understanding regarding its meaning and significance."God is Love." "Beauty is in the eye of the beholder." "What is the meaning of life?" Each of these phrases represents a lesson to be studied and learned.

Many times phrases like “God is love” are bantered around in a casual fashion. People don't take the time to study what these phrases mean, to see their importance, and to learn their proper use and value. When participating in the process of meditation your relationship with words changes. As you understand what words mean and how significant they are you become more cautious in your use of them. If the statement "I love you" has profound meaning and significance for you, then you do not say and mean it lightly. If "I love you" carries with it a shallow interpretation then your love for hot dogs and humans have equal weight, and people may actually be confused, offended, or hurt when you say you love them.

Not all meditation processes use seed-thoughts. Meditation without seed is the process of simply stilling the mind so that it can be receptive to whatever is present. There is no predetermined goal to gain insight along a certain line of thinking. Instead, you allow the spontaneous arousal of what is already present to simply be revealed to you. It should be noted that even though this is thought to be goal-less meditation, often it is not. There is value in simply being receptive to what is. But, this can include anger, hatred, violence, sedition, and a host of negative impacts which are present. And, it may not be the right time or place to be receptive to them, especially if they have become obsessive.

True, there is a time and place to become receptive to whatever feelings and thoughts are present even if they are negative. Mindfulness meditation where you develop the witness consciousness and learn to become detached and observant of whatever is there is particularly helpful along these lines. Now, you simply observe, validate, let pass, or decide how to be with whatever arises. Yet, often you must be a little more discriminative than this. Therefore, you might chose a particular orientation in your meditation as to what you want to be receptive to. This is where the use of a seed-thought is valuable.

However, at the highest level of meditation, known as contemplation, seed-thoughts drop away altogether. Remember in contemplation you are attempting to become internally quiet so that the mind, emotions, brain and nervous system become a template that reflects higher levels of light, presence, or stillness. Here you are attempting to enter into a certain state of being, more than trying to gain insight. Still, even without a seed-thought, alignment and intention established at the beginning of the meditation can be useful. That's because the alignment determines the direction of where you are going. For example, you could just as easily set an intention, or make an alignment, to head towards Italy to experience what it is like to be an Italian, or make an alignment to head towards the stars metaphorically to discover what it is like to experience yourself as a Cosmic Being.

AFFIRMATIONS & MANTRAS

An affirmation is a word, or a series of words repeated over and over again with the goal of amplifying the word so it can become manifest in your life. They are primarily tools used to recondition your mind and emotions. Not all affirmations are used as part of a meditative process. But, when used with meditation they can be significant and are more properly called a mantra. Concerning affirmations, they are as numerous as there are words in any language.Examples of affirmations can include: "Each and every day, I become joyful in every way." "From this day forward, I achieve what I set out to do." "Money is coming to me in abundance from now on." "No matter what it takes, I'll get my revenge." "God, I'm fat and ugly."

As you see, an affirmation by itself need not have spiritual value. They can be constructive or destructive, selfish or selfless in application. The premise behind the use of affirmations lies in the probability that as you repeat something over and over again, it gains the power to change your life. This is because it alters your beliefs. Words can be magical. They are capable of producing effects. If you believe something to be true in life, you help to make it come true. You begin to notice, and even to seek out, those things in life which match your perception of the truth. This goes beyond a statement of fact such as the sky is blue. It gives meaning to the fact. For example: "The sky is blue; therefore, I am happy or sad."

Let's take a basic example. "Each and every day the pounds melt away." The goal of this affirmation is to help you lose weight. If you believe you are capable of losing the pounds, you will start altering your behavior to comply with the belief. You might even begin to exercise every day. You may change your diet. You may learn more about nutrition. All of these behavioral changes increase the likelihood that the pounds will *in fact* melt away each and every day.

A difficulty arises when you repeat affirmations, but don't give them any real power. If after a month of stating "each and every day the pounds melt away" you discover you have actually gained weight, then the affirmations did not have the power to actually motivate a behavior change. Instead they became little more than magical thinking. Used as dull repetitions, affirmations end up doing the opposite then of what you intend. They can even make you lethargic, ignorant, and hypocritical in your behavior. That is why affirmations must be used with logic and care. And, to be truly effective they must engage your emotions, or be enhanced by spiritual power, not just be repeated in your mind. Why emotions? Because emotions move something into motion. And, especially when emotions are combined with intelligence and spiritual power, affirmations become easier to implement and make real.

When it comes to the use of mantras, affirmations take on a different dimension and potency. Unlike affirmations, a mantra has direct spiritual value. A mantra is not simply an ordinary word or phrase repeated over and over again. It is a spiritual principle, primordial sound or archetypal word. The meaning behind a mantra is potent. It is designed to effect a change in your spiritual psyche. Mantras are sacred. Powerful mantras have also been potencized by their repetition for thousands of years by spiritual seekers of various levels of spiritual stature. Unlike affirmations, mantras can combine visual and auditory elements.

> Unlike affirmations, a mantra has direct spiritual value. A mantra is not simply an ordinary word or phrase repeated over and over again. It is a spiritual principle, primordial sound, or archetypal word.

You begin to see how words can be used at many levels in the meditation process. For example, the word love can be a seed-thought, an affirmation, or a mantra. When used as a seed-thought, you enter into a quest to discover what love really means. As an affirmation, you hope to amplify within yourself the quality of love by repeating that you are loving so that your behaviors start to reflect more loving actions. As a mantra, you use the word love as a doorway to enter into the presence of the realm of love itself.

Remember a seed-thought is a method of seeking out the meaning of what something is. An affirmation is a means of learning how to become more of what you believe. And, a mantra is a doorway into being and recognizing that which is. Learning to understand the difference is important. For example, someone may say they are using a mantra, but if they are just repeating a phrase over and over again then in truth they are using it more like an affirmation. Or, if they are thinking with a mantra to understand its meaning, then they are using it more like a seed-thought. For this reason, some discretion is advised when claims are made regarding the use of mantras as they are only truly potent and effective when used as a doorway to consciously and with specific spiritual intention enter into a certain spiritual realm.

SUMMARY

We have just reviewed some of the components and aspects of meditation practice. In the remainder of this series the focus will now shift to expand upon these and give techniques which will assist you in developing the aforementioned skills. Proficiency in meditation will not turn you into a magical super being. It will however help you deal with your life in a more powerful, dynamic, calm, and reassured manner. For this reason everyone should be encouraged to meditate. It is not only a doorway into truth, it is a practical tool which can be utilized to help you become more of who you really are.

Location & Conditions For Practice

Meditation can be very challenging; therefore, preparation is important. Preparation helps you eliminate many obstacles that may cause needless distractions. Preparation helps beginners to start from the most advantageous position. And, it provides advanced meditators with a strong foundation when reviewing the basics.

When beginning meditation practice for the first time it is important to pick a location that accommodates you and limits distractions. Beginners are less inclined to have mastery over their physical, emotional, and mental processes. For this reason a meditative environment freed from distractions helps. This includes creating an environment where you feel physically comfortable, emotionally content, and mentally free from inner and outer intrusions. Later, as your practice accelerates resistences may be deliberately added to test your skills. But, when starting these are best avoided. Let us examine how you may do this.

FINDING A PLACE TO MEDITATE

Physical comfort varies for each individual. Some people only relax in a room free from clutter. Others are nonplused by this. Other people like an entire room dedicated to meditative practice. Others are content to carve out a small corner within a larger space. Then there are those who prefer a room to be totally empty for meditation purposes. Others find it useful to add objects that are psychologically and spiritually meaningful. Whatever the individual preference, it is important to build a sense that this room, or place, is your space. Humans, like animals have a natural territorial instinct. They like to feel that a place is theirs so they can feel at home there. If the room is familiar, if personal belongings exist within it (especially those that inspire meditation), or if the room is particularly inspirational or to your liking, it will assist your ability to feel comfortable and start to relax.

As for the actual location most people meditate best within the privacy of their homes. Some who attend a regular place of worship, may be inspired to meditate there if they are able. However, if meditation is to become a regular habit, then the space you choose needs to be easily accessible and reliable for you to use it often. At home is usually the best spot to meet these needs especially if you intend to meditate on a daily basis. As for what room in the home, it is best to pick one which allows you a sufficient amount of privacy so as not to be disturbed. If other people live with you it is even a good idea to think of placing a lock or sign on the door which prevents accidental interruptions. The room you use is also best placed away from areas where noisy activity may be taking place such as TV, recreational rooms, rooms near a busy street. If possible also choose a room which is not used by other individuals. This helps ensure that your own meditative tone remains in the place.

Whatever place you chose be sure to pay attention to possible distractions which may exist within the room itself. Ticking clocks may sound like loud gongs when you are trying to be internally silent. If you are using a clock, a digital one is best. Phones ringing in the middle of a meditation can leave you suddenly frazzled and un-nerved.Either remove the phone, or turn it off for the time being. Even setting a pager or cell phone to vibrate can be a distraction to the meditative process. If possible, turn these devises off altogether.

Before you enter your meditative space make sure other members of your household understand your intentions. Request of them that they allow you fifteen to thirty minutes of private time. Be clear what circumstances do and do not warrant interruption. By asking for the cooperation of others ahead of time, it minimizes the unexpected knocks on the door or sudden interruptions as people accidentally walk in on you. If you are embarrassed to let the people you live with know what you are doing see it as a spiritual exercise. Use your request for private time as an opportunity to tell them what you need without being offensive, condescending, or unnecessarily timid. Simply speak as if meditation is a natural thing to do, like maintaining silence in a park so you can listen to nature, or simply wanting to be alone with your thoughts. If they feel respected and not pushed aside in your desire to meditate, most people will usually honor your request for a short period of silence.

Regardless of the location you pick, it is important to find a setting which allows you to use it on a regular basis. Whenever you are trying to establish a new habit pattern it is a good to refrain from making too many changes.

Regardless of the location you pick, it is important to find a setting which allows you to use it on a regular basis. Whenever you are trying to establish a new habit pattern it is a good to refrain from making too many changes. These changes can act like excuses or distractions that prevent you from seriously attempting to do what you intend to do. If you are new to meditation, you will very likely find numerous excuses unless your motivation is strong. If the room is an appealing place for you to be in these excuses will lessen, and you will begin to look forward to meditation without forcing yourself to do so.

Once you become more skilled at meditation, you will discover the above rules begin to vary. Skilled meditators can hold their internal quiet despite outside interruptions. As you master your internal processes, you are not as sensitive to noises in or out of the room. Your concentration and level of absorption remain in tact. Likewise, the place you chose to meditate may vary. Once the habit of meditation is established, it is possible to meditate in any location you feel impelled to. Advanced meditators also know how to weave inner and outer disturbances into the fabric of their meditative state. Like drifting clouds in the sky these interruptions are simply put in the background, allowed to come and go without effecting the overall landscape you are focused upon.

THE CORRECT POSTURE FOR MEDITATION

Except when involved in relaxation exercises the best posture for meditation is one sitting up with the back erect. The reason for this is simple. Meditation is mostly a concentrated, focused, dynamic, and intuitive exercise. While engaged in it you are attempting to remain awake and alert. The normal posture when you are awake is one of sitting and standing up. When you lie down you are more tempted to fall asleep. You tend to relax and to allow your minds to drift into unconsciousness. If you are attempting to get in touch with the grounding forces of earth, simply wish to relax, or only want to let your thoughts and imagination drift, lying down is appropriate since this is what you do when you attempt to go to sleep. However, formal meditation processes preclude this. You do not want to drift off. Unless you are engaged in a formal mindfulness meditation practice you are attempting to do much more than simply watch the flow of your thoughts and feelings. Thus, it is a good idea to avoid the habit of lying down as much as possible when you have graduated beyond just the relaxation and visualization exercises.

When sitting for meditation practice you can either choose to sit on the floor or in a chair. Meditation in Eastern teachings is typically done on the floor or on a special cushion or bench. In Western mystery traditions meditation was usually practiced sitting erect in a chair. Whatever format you choose the most important thing is to be comfortable while keeping your back and spine erect. Your spine is a marvelous instrument. Through it much of your nervous system intertwines. For this reason the spine is unusually sensitive to impact. Keeping the spine flexible and with the proper curvature aids you in the proper reception of subtle energies. If your spine is damaged, if your back becomes compacted, your sensitivity likewise diminishes.

Protecting your spine through correct posture and support while sitting for meditation is vital. Since many Westerners are not accustomed to the floor sitting in a chair is usually best. Ideally, the chair should be firm, but not too rigid or soft. It should support the natural contours of the spine and accommodate your weight. While sitting in the chair, it is best to place your feet naturally onto the floor, while gently resting your palms in your lap. (Though there is a system known as mudras that instruct you to put your hands in various postures to help facilitate certain intentions and results during meditative states. For example, hands in the lap palms up symbolize receptivity and openness to the energies you are working with during meditation). Also, avoid crossing your legs and arms if it causes you circulation problems, fatigues, cramps, or causes your limbs to fall asleep easily.

If crossing your limbs is not an issue, then the choice to do so may relate to your intention during meditation. Feet on the floor symbolize your connection to the ground. If you decide to sit on the ground, the best idea is to sit cross-legged in what is referred to as the Easy Pose. When in the Easy Pose your legs rest comfortably underneath your torso in a crossed position. The most practical reason for using this posture is that it allows your weight to be supported. In advanced systems of meditation, especially in the system of Hatha Yoga, this Easy Pose is made more complex. In the Half-Lotus and Full-Lotus positions the feet are drawn up close to the body, sometimes placing each foot firmly along each side of the pelvic region. (The Half-Lotus pose anchors one leg firmly in the pelvic region while crossed. In the Full-Lotus pose, both legs are crossed with heels pressing firmly upon the pelvic region).

These advanced poses demand a greater measure of flexibility, which many people are unable to master. They also are designed to incur effects which not all people are aware of. For example, the placement of the feet along the pelvic region is designed to inhibit, or lock out, the subtle energy currents of the sexual organs. Similar to the idea of cutting off circulation, ancient meditators found that distracting sexual impulses were also cut off when pressure was applied in the groin region. This posture is therefore ideal for someone living a monastic lifestyle. It can even assist in re-directing attention away from sexual thoughts during meditation. However, if used unwisely the posture can thwart the sexual drive of those who may not have intended it to have that effect. For this reason if you chose to adopt the full-lotus posture and are uncomfortable with a drop in libido, the legs should be brought back into the Easy Pose, or you should try sitting in a chair with feet anchored on the floor.

Other ways to sit include using an ergometric chair or kneeling. The ergometric chair is an armless and backless chair. You sit on it much as you would a stool. The main difference is the angle at which the pelvis is tipped forward, and the position of the legs which rest underneath the body on a cushion of their own. The ergonomic chair is surprisingly comfortable, something you might not expect on a first impression when seeing it. If you have back difficulty, however, this choice of chair may not be the best for you as it may be more problematic for you to keep your spine erect.

When kneeling with you legs underneath you, you may also have difficulty keeping your back erect. And, you may have problems with the circulation of your calves and feet that distract you out of the deeper levels of meditation. The kneeling posture is interesting, however, because it can have the additional effect of placing your mind and emotions naturally into a certain state of reverence. For this reason kneeling can be especially helpful in worship and prayer. To understand for yourself these different subtle effects practice meditating first in a chair, then with your feet cross-legged in the Easy Pose, and then in a kneeling posture while resting on your feet. Simply observe the different mental and emotional states which arise. You might be surprised at the differences that emerge.

As mentioned lying down is not the best position for serious meditation work. Yet, it does facilitate relaxation because the weight of the body is supported by the ground. Lying down is also good for trance type fantasy journeys. These fantasy trips allow the mind to wander freely simply letting the imagination go and explore what it wants to. There is no attempt to direct or control the experience. It is more a free association exercise, random in nature. It is much like dreaming where the mind associates random images which may or may not have any meaning or significance. When it comes to concentration, directed visualization, and the higher forms of meditation lying down can cause beginners to lose their focus. They may become too relaxed, trance out, drift into dream like states, or simply cause the person to fall asleep. Thus, the true advantages of meditation are lost and the basics are never mastered.

TIPS FOR THE BODY DURING MEDITATION

No matter what meditation posture you chose, a few final tips can help you in relation to placement of your hands, eyes, head position, and how to cope with somatic antics. At first, it is important to simply do what is natural, comfortable, and whatever best helps you lift your focus of attention away from the realm of the strictly physical. Hands may rest gently in your lap with palms up, or they may rest palms down with fingers outstretched. Unless you are engaged in mudra practice the fact that you are placing your hands on an arm rest, or in your lap makes no difference. As mentioned before, mudras are specific hand gestures which are symbolic and have an underlying meaning. There are many different hand gestures you can use. These include gestures for compassion, clarity, peace of mind, balance, benevolence, to name just a few. For more information consider getting the book *Healing Mudras* by Sabrina Mesko, which is provides an excellent understanding of fifty different mudra positions.

During meditation your eyes can be open or closed. For beginners it is often easiest to keep the eyes closed. In this way the outer world of objects disappears and there is less to distract your attention. When closing your eyes for a prolonged period of time be sure to remove any contact lenses if they will tend to block the flow of oxygen to your eyes. As for closing the eyes some beginners are unaccustomed to doing so and need to watch the tendency to fall asleep at first. This can be monitored by others if you are in a group or practicing with a teacher.

When meditating with a group some people who close their eyes also feel anxious and self-conscious. They wonder what is going on with the people around them or are concerned with how they look. By being overly concerned about what others are doing during a meditation it is easy to be led away from the purpose of the meditation exercise. This can be remedied by bringing your attention back to the purpose of your meditation. A good teacher will also be able to help you overcome any self-conscious preoccupations.

When the eyes are open it is best to concentrate them in a fixed stare. There are many different beliefs of how to position the eyes. Some say you should stare at a candle, others believe you should pick a spot in front of you such as a place on the wall. Then there are systems which ask you to stare at your lap, or instruct you to gaze with your open eyes downward. They may even require you to concentrate on the tip of your nose. The advantage of open eye meditation is that it can teach you to meditate almost anywhere. Why? Because closing your eyes in a public setting may look curious to others. Simply diverting your attention while the eyes are open is less conspicuous. At the same time, open eye meditation may be difficult to learn. It can also lead to eye strain especially if you start staring and forget the natural need of the eyes to blink.

Eventually advanced meditators have facility with either open or closed eyes. One of the more difficult efforts with open eye meditation is the practice of visualization. Most people visualize easiest on a dark background. They need either a dark room or a dark environment to be able to imagine various pictures. However, the practice of visualization with the eyes open does have its advantages. For example, it allows you to interact with people, while at the same time visualizing. While you are talking with the person, you simply throw up an image in front of you, much as you would throw up a hologram. This is particularly useful in healing work.

If you wish to practice open eye visualization it is best to start by looking at a blank wall. White and black are the easiest colors to begin with. Pay attention to the lighting, making it neither too bright, nor too dim. Picture images in front of you as if you are watching them play out on the wall like a movie on a screen. With practice you can even move the object around.

When deciding what to do with your head, the best position is to look straight forward and drop your chin slightly. This is much more comfortable for your neck and will help you to avoid cramping or tiring. Resting the head backwards, perhaps onto a pillow or head rest, is not recommended. It may be relaxing, but like lying down it tends to make you drift off or go to sleep.

As for somatic antics this refers to your body's tendency

to twitch, itch, grumble, cramp up, and fall asleep. If you begin to twitch, try moving the muscle to help it relax. If you itch, simply scratch and go back to your meditation. If your stomach is grumbling, send a mental suggestion that you will feed it shortly, in about ten to twenty minutes. If you cramp up, spend some time slowly stretching the muscle. If a leg or arm falls asleep, shift its position to improve the circulation. This usually involves elevating it in the air.

> No matter what meditation posture you chose, a few final tips can help you in relation to placement of your hands, eyes, head position, and how to cope with somatic "antics."

It is my opinion that these somatic "antics" are best handled naturally and swiftly. Refusing to scratch an itch by keeping your attention elsewhere may be an interesting exercise in mind over matter. But, too often individuals end up spending their meditation absorbed with the thought of whether it is O.K. to scratch or not, and lose sight of the original intention altogether. For this reason is it best to be matter of fact about these bodily outbursts, attending briefly to them, and then returning to where you left off in your meditation.

Rhythm, Timing, and Attitude

HOW LONG TO MEDITATE

The duration or time involved for meditation varies. Often it depends on the type of meditation you are using. For most people the standard of fifteen to twenty minutes at a set period of time is recommended. Beginners often find even five minutes of meditation challenging, let alone fifteen or twenty. Often even intelligent and educated people are surprised at how undisciplined their thoughts, emotions, and physical bodies are if asked to enter into meditation. For many active people meditation appears outwardly as doing nothing. Since sustaining concentration at first is often laborious it is best to build up your capacity slowly. Master meditating for five minutes, then ten, then fifteen, then twenty. In this way you build up your discipline and prepare yourself for more rigorous work.

Eventually, you will be able to sustain your meditation practice for longer periods of time. Formal meditations can last as long as an hour or even an entire day. The ultimate goal is to learn how to be in a meditative state of mind twenty-four hours a day every day of your life. Given practice over time you will eventually achieve this. You can even learn to meditate during your sleep through certain meditative exercises that include things like lucid dreaming, or going beyond this into meditation during what is known as deep dreamless sleep.

Until one builds mastery meditating for lengthy periods of time can be dangerous. To simplify, things think of your brain as a muscle that can get cramped in attempting more than it is capable of in meditation practices. Or, to use a computer analogy consider that for some time your brain may not possess the memory, speed, or storage capacity required for sustained meditative work. This is why you must continually re-format and upgrade your brain whenever you are expanding your consciousness through meditative work. Only in this way can your receiving instrument, your brain, process meditative energies and insights correctly.

THE HABIT OF MEDITATION

To really be effective it is important to set up the habit of meditation so that a meditation rhythm begins to be established that will help you move closer to the goal of having meditation be a focus throughout your day. When establishing the habit of meditation it is best to pick a certain time of day and stay with it until the rhythm is established. Various times can be chosen. The best time is one you will stick with on a regular basis. Most frequently used times include early in the morning, mid-day, early evening, and just before bed-time.

To really be effective it is important to set up the habit of meditation so that a meditation rhythm begins to be established that will help you move closer to the goal of having meditation be a focus throughout your day.

Early Morning. Early morning meditation is best undertaken after you have been awake and active for a little while. In this way your mind is fresh, yet alert. Many people prefer to shower or exercise a little before starting their meditation. This is fine so long as your mind does not race ahead in anticipation of the day's events. If you live in a natural surrounding, morning meditation is also advantageous if done in synchronicity with the rising sun. The rising sun is an excellent symbol for the awakening of light into your mind. The sun also symbolizes the soul in some traditions, or the spirit or light within you. Meditation on the rising sun allows you to consider how the soul, spirit, or light is emerging within you during the morning hours as well.

Mid-Day. Another good time to meditate is at mid-day. Even if people do not have time for a formal meditation, mid-day is an excellent time to take a pause from the days events and consider where you are headed and what or who you really are. When the sun is uppermost in the sky as a symbol it represents the time during a day when your light is at its fullest potential. This light may be of two kinds. The highest light is that of your soul or Spirit. If this light is uppermost at mid-day, it means you are in tune with your innermost self. The lowest light, is that of your ego. If by noon this light is controlling you, you tend to be excessively ambitious and confident. This produces insensitivity and arrogance, which would best be reviewed from a higher perspective.

If your light is not bright enough at this time of day, the sun helps remind you of your spiritual identity and infuses you with qualities of courage, heart, and spiritual daring. The only difficulties with attempting regular formalized meditation at this time of day include finding the time, privacy, and space to keep the appointment regularly. If this is not possible, mid-day exercises are best done along the lines of saying a silent prayer, or simply repeating a meaningful affirmation. This strengthens the inner spiritual link without having to take the twenty to thirty minutes of private quiet time required for more extensive meditative practice.

Early Evening. Early evening meditation is probably the

second best choice of a time for regular consistent meditation. (Early morning being the best). The major task in the evening is to let go of the activities of the day as quickly as possible. If this can be done, evening meditation builds in excellent skills in coping with stress and increasing peace of mind. Again, meditation at this time can be enhanced if practiced at the time of the setting sun. Dusk symbolizes a chance to review the application of your spiritual intentions throughout the day. The sun, representing your spiritual nature, has radiated its light for at least a twelve hour period. As it sets the opportunity comes to review how you have handled your day from a spiritual level. It also gives you the chance to consider how you might carry out your spiritual intentions more effectively tomorrow. As the stars come into view they help you reflect on how the sun that you are is simply one sun amongst a multitude. This expands your sense of identity and is excellent for building in humility as you examine our relationship to others.

Late Evening. Late evening, just before retiring to bed, is usually the most difficult time period to meditate for beginners. After a long day your mind tends to be tired. When meditating you may too easily drift into dream like states instead of staying alert. Your physical fatigue often tempts you into postponing the meditative process.

If these tendencies are avoided, night time meditation assists you in examining the entire rhythm of the day. It may also be a time when the thought-waves of others are settling down. This added stillness helps your mind to be still as well. At night, an additional habit may be attempted, that of consciously preparing for the sleep process. As you enter the sleep state conscious intentions may be set as to what your dream and sleep time can accomplish for you. You begin to do this by refraining from thinking that sleep is just a time to zone out. Instead, you realize what its purpose is in your life.

In brief, deep sleep is the means by which you reconnect with your deepest identity. It is akin to entering deep levels of meditation practice on a more unconscious level. Dream, or REM, sleep is the time you are most likely to be receptive to symbolic images. Depending on your ability to be sensitive to these images, they may convey messages of profound significance. There are even those who through the practice of lucid dreaming, have learned to be awake during their dream state, consciously manipulating the content of their dreams at will. Finally, there are those who practice the habit of posing a question upon retiring so that upon awakening they might receive an insight or answer.

In order to help you with meditation at these various times throughout the day, I have actually created a CD for you called *Visualizing YOU Throughout the Day.* Here I guide you through five different meditation processes that can help you establish the habit pattern of meditation, and help you remember who you are as a spiritual being throughout each and every day of your life. The CD can be found for sale at my www.doctorlisalove.com website.

FREQUENCY OF MEDITATION

The last consideration under this heading is how often to meditate. Ideally meditation is best done every day. This is easily accomplished if you make it a priority and structure your life so there is time to include it. When meditation becomes an everyday habit you tend to feel more in charge of your life. You are more relaxed. You handle difficult situations better. You are more aware of yourself and how to correct your reactions during stressful situations. Also, you have been able to dress rehearse life scenarios in your mind's eye (often through visualizations) so you are confident should difficult situations manifest themselves again in your life.

> If you are becoming too passive, zoned out, over-stimulated, confused, or disconnected from everyday life through meditation practices, or becoming attached to altered states of consciousness you may want to cut back on or stop your meditation practice.

At times, it should be stated, it may not be good to meditate on a daily basis, or even at all. This statement often surprises people who have no understanding that meditation can actually have drawbacks attached to it. For example, if you are becoming too passive, zoned out, over-stimulated, confused, or disconnected from everyday life through meditation practices, or becoming attached to altered states of consciousness you may want to cut back on or stop your meditation practice. That is because meditation might only reinforce inertia and indifference to everyday life events.

Remember meditation as a practice is not intended to lead you away from involvement with the world. On the contrary, it should help you cope more effectively in it. In this way you can "be in the world, but not be of it" to quote a Christian phrase. Suffice it to say for now that mediation like everything in life has the potential if abused to create some difficulties. If this is the case practitioners are invited to temporarily cut back or abstain from practice until they are more focused, grounded, and centered in their daily lives.

ATTITUDE & MEDITATION WORK

There is a story about a man who went to Japan seeking enlightenment. There he met a Zen master of some spiritual renown. Anxious to learn the secret to enlightenment the man implored to the Zen master to teach him. Agreeing to the request, the Zen master asked the man to walk over to a pool of water and gaze into it. The man did so and as he was looking into the water, suddenly the Zen master grabbed the man's head and submerged it forcefully under the water. Gasping for air and attempting to escape the fierce hold the Zen master had on him, the man finally surrendered helplessly to his impending fate of seemingly being drowned by a crazy person.

Just as the man began to welcome death, the Zen master suddenly yanked the man's head up and out of the water. At first the man simply sputtered and did his best to take in as much oxygen as his body would allow. As he came to, the man looked at the Zen master with glazed eyes and then angrily inquired as to why the Zen master would do such a crazy thing. The Zen master simply looked at the man with a deep wise stare. "Because," the Zen master replied. "When you want enlightenment as much as you wanted to breathe air when you were under the water, you will find it."

Like anything in life you achieve the most success in something if you truly want it. When you really desire something there is a great deal of momentum and energy that accompanies it. You do not need to force yourself or talk yourself into it, because you find it joyful, exciting, fun, and adventuresome to participate in. If you approach meditation in this fashion, you are much more likely to achieve success. You will be less likely to build up a thought-form that meditation is boring, tedious, hard work, and has no real purpose. The section on benefits of meditation is meant to help arouse your enthusiasm for this practice. Reviewing this section and listing the benefits on paper increases motivation and helps you progress through the more rigorous aspects of meditation until they become easy to perform bringing fruit and reward.

Another helpful attitude is one of deep love and reverence. In the deepest sense meditation is a spiritual act and is communal in nature. This communion relates to your self, your conception of God, and your contact with spiritual teachers. Also, the more you love something, the easier you apply ourselves. If each meditation period starts with a brief affirmation of its spiritual intention, it will assist you. This intention may be to become a better person, or it may relate to your intent to better the lives of those around you. Such an attitude speeds up your development in meditation allowing you to accomplish much more in a shorter period of time.

At the highest level, meditation is best used as an act of service. As you transcend thinking only of yourself, your needs, and your desires, your meditation time lets you penetrate more deeply into the problems of others, your community, and the planet as a whole. Not that you will always solve these problems, but you will gain insights which facilitate wisdom in coping. You will also mature your capacities for nurturance and compassion as you spend time each day considering the needs of another. Over time this effects the ways that you relate to others whether you are absorbed in a systematic meditation or not!

Meditating With Groups, Teachers, Or Alone

Meditation is primarily a personal journey. No one else can tell you how to live your life, what you should think, or how you should respond. The goal of meditation is similar then to self-actualization in that it helps you actualize the powers of your true self and deepen your appreciation for the divine. The more you can learn to direct your life with wisdom, the easier it will be to serve the greater whole. Paradox-ically, though meditation is engaged in internally and is therefore an individual process, in many ways it is a group process as you shift your focus away from your own personal problems, and involve yourself with the needs of others. That is also why when a group of people are likewise concerned with the good of the whole, though they may be focused internally, together as they are meditating especially along specific lines of meditation, they are much more potent when meditating together than when meditating alone. That is how group and individual meditation can both play an important part in all our lives.

MEDITATING WITH A GROUP

Whenever you are with a group of people you are carried along by their momentum. For your benefit or detriment the group influences the way you think, feel, and act. A group either empowers you by giving you more opportunities and challenges, or diminishes you by providing too many obstacles to allow for your free thought and self-expression. Group work can also be deceptive. Because a group has the power to sustain and enhance your efforts you may not be as likely to see your limitations. In any group it is natural to ride the wave of the group's momentum. In meditative groups a focused group mind has the power to heighten your senses and intuition. This can be an exhilarating experience. But, apart from the group this momentum may quickly die. Left alone you may now find yourself lacking in focus, intensity, and mastery. To balance this you need to understand the necessity of individual work carried out within any group effort. Thus, group and individual meditation work really belong together.

The advantages of group meditation are numerous. Groups lend strength to your meditative efforts. The concentrated mind of a group naturally pulls the minds of individuals into a sharper focus. Groups also provide a fertile ground in the way of insights which are invoked during meditative practice. Another way they serve is in providing challenges to the individual. They reveal weak and strong points in the individual make-up, which if handled well accelerates individual personal and spiritual growth. Finally, groups lend emotional support and companionship along the path. This diminishes personal isolation and tends to strengthen a collective world view. In turn individuals assist groups by taking initiative in the way of leadership. They help broaden the group talent base and increase its potency.

Not all relations between groups and individuals are positive. A complex set of unhealthy dynamics can arise. These often imitate destructive patterns that are carried over from an individual's previous relations with groups in particular with their early family unit. One of the most disruptive patterns is overdependency and group symbiosis. When you lose your individual focus in a group, you easily succumb to gullibility, domination, and sheepish behavior. Instead of strengthening the individual's reasoning process, or group members can weaken it by insisting that the individual does not ask questions and obeys group leaders as the ultimate authority.

This stifles individual initiative or blocks individual talent if they are seen as too confrontive in the eyes of insecure group members. Individuals may also become victims of other's petty jealousies and ambitions. Instead of finding a secure haven where they feel they can blossom and grow into spiritual maturity, the person feels manipulated and crushed. Usually when groups are not flexible enough to permit individual advancement it begins the process of crystallization and decay.

As this happens individual members of the group may rebel and break off to find a way to express their creative and spiritual needs more effectively. In turn the meditative potency and creative spiritual energy of the group drops away. All that remains are meaningless texts turned into doctrines, dogmatic leaders and repetitive ritual practices with no life or vitality.

Individuals can also pose a danger to a meditative group. When the individual fails to see the value of the group, or only wants to play a leadership role in groups he or she is involved in, difficulties emerge. The individual risks becoming ego-maniacal, imbalanced, and tyrannical in disposition. The individual may also develop a fanciful spiritual belief system making unsubstantiated claims which have never been tested objectively in the light of the overall whole.

Examples of such claims include deifying oneself, professing to have performed miracles (which no one may have witnessed), or other non-sensible claims. Individuals can also disrupt a group due to overenthusiasm with their sincere intentions. They take on too much, are indiscriminate, or overstep boundaries without knowing it. It is wise practice for any newcomer to a group to go through a probationary period. During this time, the individual is tested as to sincerity of commitment and merit. The group is likewise tested as to their ability to compassionately and wisely support individual differences and needs. If both pass the process, the strength and spiritual integrity is enhanced.

MEDITATING ALONE

Meditating alone is important whether or not you join a group. By building meditation skills on your own you demonstrate your mastery of them. You test the strength and clarity of your insights, the poise and calm of your emotions, and the intelligent and dynamic drive of your actions. You prove spiritual principles are more than just theory as you put them into everyday practice. You build in the drive and discipline based upon an internalized momentum to lead a spiritual life. Having mastered these skills they are your own. No one can take them away because they are absorbed into your very essence.

The difficulty when you only chose solitary meditation lies in succumbing to self-deception. Your spiritual mastery is tested in the fiery furnace of group interaction. Anyone can make claims as to his or her spiritual status. It is much more difficult to prove that spirituality by behaving in wise, compassionate, and skillfuls ways with others. It is easy to make great claims to fame when no one is around to challenge them. It is humbling to attempt to do so when in the presence of true spiritual masters.

Isolated meditation can also make you more self-centered. If you remain alone you benefit very few people. In a sense you become a glutton hoarding wealth and wisdom to yourself without allowing for an avenue of expression. You forget that a true spiritual path involves service at some level. This is rendered in many ways such as: organizing food for the hungry, formulating insights in a book, finding cures for medical conditions, raising a healthy family, beautifying the environment through music or art, running an ethical business, making a scientific discovery, and so forth. Without this intention for creative output meditation revelations are temporary and fruitless. That is why insight alone is not enough. At some point those insights need to be put into good use.

The question of whether to meditate alone or in a group then is really one of balance, purpose, and skill. Both can be beneficial. Both need to be mastered if one is to have a well rounded experience. Both offer opportunities and challenges which continue to strengthen and test you as to how many of the benefits from meditation you are reaping, and as to which steps you need to take next to further your growth. Both are a necessary part of your spiritual journey.

> When looking for a teacher to follow, it is useful to keep in mind that the ideal teacher speaks more from experience, and less from theory. Anyone can pick up a book and dictate to you how to fly an airplane. Only a pilot can let you know what it is really like.

USING A TEACHER

Similar to our review of group and individual dynamic, we benefit in spiritual practice both from studying with a teacher and in being self-taught. Especially in the beginning of meditation practice most people need a teacher. A teacher is advantageous, not just for the knowledge he or she possesses, but for the experience he or she has accumulated in mastering meditative skills. A teacher conveys the life of a teaching. When learning from them more of our senses our engaged. There is a greater opportunity for the unexpected and the creative to emerge. There is also the advantage of having the teacher's wisdom and experience applied specifically to your stage of developmental needs.

Having a good teacher is both an honor and an opportunity. When mentored by a teacher your growth accelerates. You benefit from the clarity of the teacher's mind. You are enhanced by the stability of his or her emotions, and the dynamic activity that energizes his or her physical environment. You also get direct exposure to the depth, breadth, and inclusiveness of the teacher's spiritual nature and life experience. The right teacher is either a living demonstration of the role model you are striving to become; or, he or she confronts you with prejudgments and blocks in your psyche which need to be mastered. A good teacher also allows for his or her humanity and does not cover up weaknesses with deception or philosophical tenants that rationalize hypocritical behavior.

When looking for a teacher to follow, it is useful to keep in mind that the ideal teacher speaks more from experience, and less from theory. Anyone can pick up a book and dictate to you how to fly an airplane. Only a pilot can let you know what it is really like. A good teacher is authentic. If the teacher has only theory to offer you, then you should know that. If a teacher has life experience, then this should be made public also. The spiritual teacher especially needs to walk the talk. To tell students to behave one way, and then have the teacher hypocritically make excuses to do otherwise, is a major danger that signals to all students that this is one teacher to be avoided.

A good teacher is basically a role model of what he or she is speaking of. In all life affairs, a spiritual teacher puts the principles of meditation practice to work. There is no excuse for having good public relations, while family members, friends, and intimates are treated rudely. Often the true test of spirituality begins with how we treat the people closest to us. They know us as we really are. If they are treated badly, as teachers we may still be an inspiration to others, but there should be some open questioning as to how much we live the teaching versus just talk about it.

Some times in your enthusiasm to find a teacher you may ignore discretion and be attracted to teachers who are not the best for us. The teacher and student interaction is a very delicate one. Whenever anyone claims to be involved in religious or spiritual work a number of dangers can arise either on the part of the student or the teacher. Some of these difficulties are the result of direct character defects in the teachers involved.

Others add up to primarily incompatibility or a lack of experience. Whenever a teacher and student first intersect there is the immediate opportunity for false impressions to arise. When a remote teaching setting is involved (where teacher and student have very little interaction) typical problems involve a tendency to misperceive or glamorize either the teacher or student. On the part of the teacher, if he or she is too distant, too impersonal, too uninvolved with the individual's progress a danger arises in that the teacher can not properly assess the impact the teachings are having upon the student.

Certain meditations are designed to produce certain effects. Not every person is meant to use certain forms of meditation practice. If a teacher gives techniques and fails to properly prepare or assess the readiness of the student, the teacher is partially at fault if certain techniques have adverse effects. On the flip side, it is common for newcomers to spiritual practice to expect too much out of their teachers. They idealize their teachers, fail to consider the teacher's limitations and weaknesses, and in doing so set themselves up for disillusionment and disappointment later on.

Alternatively, if the teacher becomes too intimate in students' lives then other difficulties can occur. The teacher may become tyrannical directing the student's every move and suffocating individual expression. The teacher may become dependent needing the student for adoration, financial support, and encouragement. The teacher may over-personalize the relationship confusing boundaries and becoming emotionally, and sometimes even sexually involved in the student's life. Because the teacher knows the student more intimately the teacher can wound the student more deeply should he or she slip into judgment, criticism, or jealousy of the student. This can create significant tension and turn into a control and power trip which both teacher and student may find it difficult to extricate themselves from. (Note: A great book to help you understand the problems of teachers taking advantage of students, especially sexually is *Sex and the Spiritual Teacher: Why it Happens, When It's a Problem, and What We All Can Do* by Scott Edelstein).

For the student, if they come to know a teacher too intimately it can quickly create fear, tension and disrespect. If the student has been taken advantage of and is afraid to speak up, the student needs to find support, often outside of the group, to help him or her cope. On the flip side if the student becomes too demanding and disrespectful of the teacher, he or she may take advantage of the teacher's weaknesses in an attempt to become better than the teacher in an egotistical way. In emphasizing the teacher's short comings, the student may too rapidly discount what strengths the teacher has to offer. Students may also normalize relations too quickly, acting as if they have the same amount of knowledge and experience in only a few short weeks of learning, whereas the teacher might have had a few decades. Finally, students may attempt to make teachers dependent upon them as a way of encouraging their special position in relation to the teaching or teacher they are involved with.

A special note. There is a tradition, known as the crazy wisdom, which should be mentioned at this stage. In this approach, the teacher deliberately acts contrary to your expectations of what spiritual behavior should be. Thus, a spiritual teacher may cuss, indulge to excess, and be otherwise offensive, as a planned tactic for testing how spiritually poised and wise you remain when confronted with these contradictions. Since the crazy wisdom can so easily be a cover up for offensive and unstable people posing as religious teachers, it is usually discouraged by most cultures and spiritual traditions.

If you meet a crazy wisdom teacher, they are best judged by the impact they are having on their students. If their students are becoming less judgmental of the flaws in themselves and others, and are learning to overcome their addictions and abusive behaviors, the "crazy wisdom" tactic of paradox is working. If students are themselves beginning to justify abusive, offensive, and addictive behaviors, the "crazy wisdom" approach is being misapplied, and is best left behind very quickly. Again refer to *Sex and the Spiritual Teacher: Why it Happens, When It's a Problem, and What We All Can Do* by Scott Edelstein to give you guidance of how to cope along these lines.

LEARNING MEDITATION ON YOUR OWN

At times gaining access to a good teacher may not be possible for you. This forces you to develop on an individual level whether you wish to or not. Numerous reasons may exist as to why you cannot find a proper teacher. One may have to do with life circumstances (fate or karma as it is sometimes called). You may not live near a teacher. The time or money necessary to enter into an internship may not be available. Family responsibilities may keep you away. Unfinished business such as completing previously initiated plans may prevent you. All of these impediments can only be rectified once a window of opportunity arises for us and lets us know the time has come to begin working with a teacher.

Other reasons may include incompatibility with teachers who are accessible. Not every teacher is right for everyone. There may be personality differences which cause more friction in the relationship than you can currently manage. The teacher may not have the time for you, or may teach in a fashion too unfamiliar to you. You may find yourself more advanced in understanding than the teacher, something you did not originally expect. All of these may cause you to continue a course of self-study, even though your real intentions may be otherwise.

Self-study can be rewarding nevertheless. Advantages of learning on your own include being able to set your pace. It helps those who undertake it to achieve a certain degree of inner strength and self-reliance when it comes to spiritual matters. There is less of a likelihood to rely upon others to ascertain what is best for you. This means you develop an inner sensitivity to your needs and own inner impulses as to which is the best way for you to go. Naturally, your views of yourself need to be monitored for distortion. If you truly possess the wisdom to let life and others be a mirror to you, then the book of life itself becomes your teacher in the guise of your everyday interactions with family members, friends, co-workers, and life overall.

> As a final recommendation, most of us need to allow for a cyclic flow between working independently and with a teacher. There are periods when a teacher and student may interact intensively together, and periods when they should remain apart.

As a final recommendation, most of us need to allow for a cyclic flow between working independently and with a teacher. There are periods when a teacher and student may interact intensively together, and periods when they should remain apart. This cyclic flow sustains the joy involved in teacher student interaction, but also maintains enough distance that over-dependency and reliance upon each other does not become protracted. It also allows for better clarity as to the real strengths and weaknesses of the teachers and students involved. In this way the interaction progresses from parent-child to adult-adult dimensions.

By keeping in mind the need for every student to achieve

spiritual independence, the teacher prepares in advance for the inevitable day when the student is recognized as having grown up. If this rite of passage is not undergone consciously, or is suppressed, even the most enduring and endearing student-teacher relationship can falter on the shores of bitterness, disillusionment, and resentment. It is absolutely vital therefore for teacher and student to know how to handle the evolution of their relationship in a way which fosters maturity and respect. In the truest sense teacher and student enter into friendship. As both seek to contribute the fruits of their meditative and spiritual insights to others in the world, a bond remains between them which allows for mutual support and understanding. Thus, all benefit from having touched the lives of former teacher and former student as they walk in friendship together.

Creating a Sacred Space for Meditation

Meditative practice is best sustained if viewed as a sacred experience whereby you can contact what is most essential, loving, and peaceful within your inner most Self. Though at the height of proficiency meditation can be practiced anywhere, for many people its practice is enhanced by the use of a ritualized space set aside specifically for meditative purposes. (Note: when you ritualize something it becomes a prescribed way of doing something, which in turn becomes a habit pattern).

> Your sacred space will vary from others according to your individual aspirations. The amount of space you need will vary depending upon how much space you have to work with.

THE ROLE OF SACRED SPACE

When you meditate you are attempting to concentrate the mind, calm the emotions, and orient your physical brain towards a certain state of awareness. For many, this is best done only in a space with limited distractions. These distractions can occur in a variety of ways. Distractions may be generated by other people in the guise of their words and actions. Distractions may come from outer stimuli in the way of obtrusive sounds, smells, sights, and so forth. Distractions may also be of an inner nature coming from your own thoughts and feelings. On a subtle level, distractions can also take place in the form of an inner sensitivity to other people's thoughts and feelings.

Finally, distractions may arise from setting up certain patterns or associations that interfere with the meditative state of mind. For example, if the room you are using for meditation is that same room you use for business purposes some difficulties may arise since being in that space may remind you or unfinished pending work that you are being reminded that you need to attend to. In order to meditate without distraction there you may need to spend extra time clearing your business related thoughts and feelings, before you can shift towards your intended meditative focus.

Another reason a sacred space may be important is because rooms and environments all have certain associations connected to them. These associations are built mainly by the type of activities you are engaging in within any space or room. But, they are also built by the layout of the space itself including: the arrangement of furnishings; the use of color; the placement of icons in the way of pictures or items with symbolic significance for us; and the way you consciously or unconsciously work within the space. The use of Feng Shui is built on the premise of arranging the space and items within it to make it more harmonious and to help certain spaces reflect better certain intentions. When it comes to creating a sacred space it is also important that the space invokes the sacred, is a space you can relax and feel restored in, helps to reflect your innermost self, and in a sense is a mini temple, in seems holy (or whole making) at some level.

SETTING UP YOUR SACRED SPACE

Your sacred space will vary from other spaces according to your individual aspirations. The amount of space you need will vary depending upon how much space you have to work with. On the simplest level this space only needs to comprise enough room to simply sit and be. On a more complex level, it will give you enough room to feel at home in the space of your body and help you easily master your thoughts, feelings, and body in such a way you can enter into deeper and more profound meditative states.

This ideal aside, limited space can be worked with in the following ways. First, you could establish a corner of a room and designate it as your sacred space. In this corner, you could place images essential to your sense of divinity in the way of scenes of nature, pictures of saints or meaningful teachers, colors soothing and uplifting to our psyches, or other symbols in the way of patterns, shapes, or forms. To work best the space should be kept clean and not used for any other intention. As you work with the space, everything within the space should be consciously chosen and be a meaningful reflection of our spiritual selves.As the space is entered and exited a psychological association of moving into a reverential state of being can be kept. This maintains the purity of the environment and helps to reinforce our meditative focus.

The second means in which you can work with a limited space is to simply chose a specific rug or mat to be used specifically for meditative purposes. At one point in my life I had to resort to this method as I lived in a small space with a roommate who occupied the same space at times. The mat then became the "sacred space" and was available wherever I chose to use it. The use of a mat is also ideal if you are also involved in travel. Sacred items can be rolled up into the mat and transported within the mat's protective aura. As the mat is unrolled the sacred items may be placed before one as spiritual reminders.

The use of a larger space really varies little from the use of a smaller one. The difference is simply one of having more room to play with. This allows you to place furniture, or larger items, in a harmonious way within the space itself. Here you may also set up an alter placing candles, bells, flowers, incense, sacred art objects, and personal mementos there that help to invoke and reflect unity and wholeness. You may also consider the addition of power objects or "magical tools." These can include a Tibetan Vajra Dorje thunderbolt emblem, a Native American peace pipe, rosary beads, a special ring, and so forth. Also, lighting is something you may consciously play with in the way of light, dark, or colored light effects. Each item you use may be intuitively picked, but it also helps if you consciously know the intended purpose behind whatever you chose to use.

> Sometimes the best way to access Spirit and move into a sacred space is to get away and go to a specific area like a retreat center, church, synagogue, temple, mosque or place in nature that is designated as a sacred site or invokes the state of meditation because meditation activities are regularly performed there.

MAINTAINING YOUR SACRED SPACE

Whatever you decide to do with your sacred space, the most important ingredient is you attitude and approach towards your sacred space. Consider your space a holy temple. If possible, protect it from interfering influences without becoming attached or fanatical. Approach your space with respect. If need be even shower or change your clothing before entering your space to reinforce setting the right mood of getting ready to do something sacred.

If your space cannot be protected from outside influences use rituals to clear it out. This may include the regular cleaning of your space, clearing the energy there with sage or incense, or visualizations of wind, sun, or water purifying your space. Or, it may include the use of hand gestures, movements, affirmations, chants, sacred songs, or other techniques which reinforce psychologically the purity of the space around you. In conclusion, the advantage of creating a sacred space for meditative purposes is that it helps to reinforce and remind you of your most essential self. How you treat your space is often likewise a reflection of how you relate to, view, and treat this Self. Tend it with care that it may grow in beauty, power, strength, and joy.

Sacred Space Exercise. If you have not already done so, establish for yourself a sacred meditative space. Review the list above and determine how you may best do this. Remember to chose a method which is best adapted to your lifestyle, needs, and the amount of, and kind of space you have to work with. Also, consider how much the space may or may not have distracting influences around it. Ideally, create a space which offers you the least resistance.

MEDITATION RETREATS

Sometimes the best way to access Spirit and move into a sacred space is to get away and go to a specific area like a retreat center, church, synagogue, temple, mosque or place in nature that is designated as a sacred site or invokes the state of meditation because meditation activities are regularly performed there. While visiting these places you can do so in an informal or formal way. When done informally you simply go to one of these sacred spots and pray or meditate for whatever amount of time is meaningful to you. When done formally you may go for a specific reason and even be amongst a group of people with exercises being led by a spiritual teacher.

You may also be following a structured meditation program. Regardless of whether meditation work is formal or informal it is good to attempt to get to sacred sites or places on a regular basis. And, it is especially helpful to do whenever you are going through a stressful or transitional part of your life (such as the loss of a job, a health crisis, a death, divorce, or end of a significant relationship).

In conclusion, now that you understand the benefits and various practices of meditation it is hoped that meditation becomes a regular part of your life. And, if you want further support you are welcome to contact me, Dr. Lisa Love, or utilize any of the references listed in this book.

ABOUT DR. LISA LOVE

Dr. Lisa Love is the best-selling author of *Beyond the Secret* and a counselor with five degrees in Marriage, Family, and Child Counseling, as well as Spiritual Psychology and Transpersonal Psychology. Using her extensive training and experience she helps others through individual and group coaching programs as well as writes, speaks and gives workshops on joy, spirituality, love, relationships, dating and the spiritual use of the law of attraction. She also helps people REACH to become *Rapidly Evolving Agents for Changing Humanity.*™ She does this by helping them make dramatic breakthroughs so they can live more soulful and truly meaningful lives. Mostly she helps her clients cultivate empathy and compassion for all of their life experience so they can live in a state of joy, peace of mind, health and love.

- Founder
  - *REACH programs*
  - *LoveMovies!*
  - *Soul to Spirit*
- Author
  - *Beyond the Secret*
  - *Feeling Good & Living Great*
  - *How NOT to Love Yourself*
  - *Meditation: The Path to Peace*
  - *Attracting Real Love*
- Former
  - *Match.com* dating advisor
  - *America Online* teacher
- Websites & Social Media:
  - www.doctorlisalove.com
  - www.facebook.com/drlisalove
  - www.twitter.com/doctorlisalove
  - www.youtube.com/doctorlisalove
- Media and radio personality
- *LiveAdvice.com* top counselor
- Syndicated columnist
- Counselor and coach with over 25 years experience
- Owner of 5 psychology & counseling degrees

Beyond the Secret

Spiritual Power
& the Law of Attraction

By Dr. Lisa Love

The greatest secret isn't know how to wish; it's knowing what to wish for!

"Reading this book will help you find happiness and when you do, you will be a success." — Bernie Siegel, MD

A best-selling book now in 5 languages *Beyond the Secret*, explains how to use the law of attraction in a spiritually powerful way. The Law of Attraction tells us that we can have anything we want. Or does it? How do we know if we're using it for the right purpose? Lisa Love answers these questions, drawing upon insights she received during her own spiritual quest. She explains the difference between using the Law in an egotistical rather than a spiritual way showing how the Law of Attraction can be a tool for spiritual growth, psychological integration, and, ultimately, connecting with Spirit.

- **Best-selling book** now in its **3rd Printing**!
- Learn the **Ten Step Process** that helps you attract what Spirit most wants for you to have in life.
- Discover how to attract and transform **"you" into "YOU"** or your higher spiritual self so your wishes and desires are anchored in spiritual principles.
- Get access to **over 30 practical techniques** that help you manifest what you want in life in a spiritual way.
- Discover your **spiritual purpose** for being here.
- Start NOW to attract more of what Spirit really wants for to **live a truly loving and fulfilling life!**

To Order Book Please Visit: www.doctorlisalove.com

Feeling Good & Living Great

How Handling Any Feeling Well Helps You Live a Better Life

By Dr. Lisa Love

Improve your life by releasing the positive potential of every feeling.

Living great isn't hard! It all depends on how you feel about your life. Discovery how every feeling has a gift to give you and all feelings can become your friends when you transform feelings into their higher state. Anger, sorrow, jealousy, confusion, fear and happiness are all there for a reason. There are no good and bad feelings. So start now to use any feeling in a positive way to improve your life so you can feel good and live great right now!

1. Learn how to turn your:
    - Anger into Energy — to make the changes you need to.
    - Sorrow into Compassion — by increasing your empathy for self and others.
    - Fear into Love — by gaining knowledge and wisdom to handle life well.
    - Confusion into Clarity — giving you a positive direction in life.
    - Jealousy into Fulfillment — through confidence that you can have what you want.
    - Happiness into Joy — where you feel good by doing good for yourself and others.
2. Discover how to create an "Emotional Rescue Kit" that you can pull out and use quickly when you lose it emotionally bringing yourself back into balance and harmony.
3. Find out how to attract more of what you want because your emotions no longer get in the way.

How NOT to Love Yourself

Misguided Teachings From the Princess Realms

By Dr. Lisa Love

You Can Learn to Love Yourself, If You Learn At Last What NOT to Do!

Discover the mistakes nine fairy tale princesses make in their desperate quest for love. Then learn how not to make these mistakes yourself to create a true chance for a happy ever after full of *real* love, by learning how to really love yourself.

Here is just some of what you will learn in this book...

- Change your focus from putting others first to **putting yourself first** so by loving yourself so you can love others.
- Stop sleep walking through life waiting for your "prince" to come and learn **how to get conscious so you can lead a happy full life** instead.
- Stop playing dumb or naïve out of fear of facing the world, and **develop the maturity and wisdom you need to protect yourself** and surround yourself with loving people.
- Remove the tendency to give away your many talents and change yourself unfairly in an attempt to attract a partner so that you **respect your true talents and gifts** and attract someone who love you for you!
- No longer tolerate beastly behaviors in men by making excuses for them, and **learn to teach others to treat you well** loving yourself enough to attract real love to you.
- Discover ways you may be unwittingly giving your power away to others, and **learn to retain your personal power** so that you can live the life you are meant to.
- Find other ways to cope with life besides checking out in destructive ways so that you can **courageously face reality and live a life that is truly meaningful and free.**
- And, much, much, more!

To Order Book Please Visit: www.doctorlisalove.com

Attracting Real Love

5 Simple Steps for Getting the Love You Want

By Dr. Lisa Love

You Are About to Experience All the Love You Really Want to Feel....

No more heartbreak, loneliness, uncertainty, or disappointment -- just love, *real* love from now on. How? By changing your focus from finding someone out there to love you to putting the focus on thoroughly loving yourself. And, by learning what love really is so you can attract it to yourself.

It's true, most people don't have love in their lives, because they confuse love for lust, infatuation, addiction, neediness, codependency, and even abuse. But, it doesn't have to be that way when you know love really is and how to attract it to.

Here is just some of what you will learn in this book...

- It will reveal to you **how to become a real "lover" of yourself and others**.
- It will clearly help you **understand "false" versus "real" love** on love on all levels: spiritual, personal, mental, emotional, physical, and sexual.
- It will show you **how love is deeply connected to attachment and intimacy**. In fact, the lack of both of these in your life in an empowering and healthy way is typically the major root cause behind all disappointing experiences in the realm of love.
- As you continue to understand what real love is, you will also **get a new awareness of the role of romance as viewed by men, and also by women.**
- And, if your present relationship is in trouble, or you have just lost one, this book gives **practical advise on how to radically improve your relationship.**

To Order Book Please Visit: www.doctorlisalove.com

Meditation

The Path to Peace

By Dr. Lisa Love

This book is a summary of my years of practicing and teaching meditation to students locally as a teacher of meditation online through *America Online's* Online Campus.

Early in my life I discovered the many enormous benefits of meditation. And, I discovered it was a way to reveal your true spiritual identity, calm and focus your mind, and master your emotions so they are tranquil and peaceful. That is why I have practiced and even taught various forms of meditation practices for decades. At one point I even meditated four hours straight a day for a period of two years. This extensive spiritual practice even led me an in-depth understanding of just how far meditation practice can take you in discovery your true self.

- Get a clear understanding of **What Meditation Is** in both the classical and modern definition of it.
- Learn the **Eight Benefits of Meditation** that come about when you use various meditation techniques and how they can help you at all levels (spiritually, personally, mentally, emotionally, vitally, physically).
- Discover various **Types of Meditation Practice** so you can choose the meditation that is best for you.
- Find out how various practice can aid the **Various Levels of Your Being** (spiritually, personally, mentally, emotionally, vitally, physically).
- Know what is required in the way of **Meditation Aids** including setting up the right location and conditions for your meditation practice.
- **Get Started for Meditation Practice** in an effortless way so it becomes beneficial and easy for you.
- Get training in **Meditation Exercises** that can give you the best foundation for beginning, intermediate, and advanced meditation practices.

To Order Book Please Visit: www.doctorlisalove.com

REACH Programs

By Dr. Lisa Love

- Are you ready to be free?
- Are you are ready to change your life?
- Are you ready to embrace yourself and others with love and compassion?
- Are you ready to rid yourself of limitations preventing you from being who you *really* are and accomplishing what you are here for?
- Are you ready to **REACH** - to become a ***Rapidly Evolving Agent for Changing Humanity™?***

If so, join others who are dedicating themselves to a new way of living based on increased conscious awareness of self and others resulting in a culture of compassion, unity, empathy, harmony, and love. Discover how powerful you can be, and how much more joyful you will feel when you integrate all aspects of who you are.

Seven Main REACH Programs

- Conscious Security - Trusting Life to Provide for You
- Conscious Pleasure: Enjoying Life in Healthy Ways
- Conscious Power—Living With Vigor to Fulfill Your Life Purpose
- Conscious Loving: Using Real Love to Cultivate Loving Relationships
- Conscious Communication: Standing in Integrity & Truth
- Conscious Vision: Creating a Life of Peace & Love
- Conscious Unity: Experiencing Oneness as the Essence of Love

Trainings happen individually, in group format, online, and in person. Join us!

To Learn More Please Visit: www.doctorlisalove.com

www.ingramcontent.com/pod-product-compliance
Lightning Source LLC
LaVergne TN
LVHW021500080426
835509LV00018B/2352
* 9 7 8 0 6 1 5 4 8 7 9 9 1 *